JAMESTOWN ED

Timed Readings Plus
in Social Studies

BOOK 5

**25 Two-Part Lessons with Questions for
Building Reading Speed and Comprehension**

Glencoe

New York, New York   Columbus, Ohio   Chicago, Illinois   Peoria, Illinois   Woodland Hills, California

JAMESTOWN EDUCATION

 Glencoe

The *McGraw-Hill* Companies

ISBN: 0-07-845803-X

Send all queries to:
Glencoe/McGraw-Hill
8787 Orion Place
Columbus, OH 43240-4027

3 4 5 6 7 8 9 10 021 08 07 06 05

CONTENTS

To the Student

    Reading Faster and Better   2

    Mastering Reading Comprehension   3

    Working Through a Lesson   7

    Plotting Your Progress   8

To the Teacher

    About the Series   9

    Timed Reading and Comprehension   10

    Speed Versus Comprehension   10

    Getting Started   10

    Timing the Reading   11

    Teaching a Lesson   11

    Monitoring Progress   12

    Diagnosis and Evaluation   12

Lessons   13–112

Answer Key   114–115

Graphs   116–118

You probably talk at an average rate of about 150 words a minute. If you are a reader of average ability, you read at a rate of about 250 words a minute. So your reading speed is nearly twice as fast as your speaking or listening speed. This example shows that reading is one of the fastest ways to get information.

The purpose of this book is to help you increase your reading rate and understand what you read. The 25 lessons in this book will also give you practice in reading social studies articles and in preparing for tests in which you must read and understand nonfiction passages within a certain time limit.

Reading Faster and Better

Following are some strategies that you can use to read the articles in each lesson.

Previewing

Previewing before you read is a very important step. This helps you to get an idea of what a selection is about and to recall any previous knowledge you have about the subject. Here are the steps to follow when previewing.

Read the title. Titles are designed not only to announce the subject but also to make the reader think. Ask yourself questions such as What can I learn from the title? What thoughts does it bring to mind?

What do I already know about this subject?

Read the first sentence. If they are short, read the first two sentences. The opening sentence is the writer's opportunity to get your attention. Some writers announce what they hope to tell you in the selection. Some writers state their purpose for writing; others just try to get your attention.

Read the last sentence. If it is short, read the final two sentences. The closing sentence is the writer's last chance to get ideas across to you. Some writers repeat the main idea once more. Some writers draw a conclusion—this is what they have been leading up to. Other writers summarize their thoughts; they tie all the facts together.

Skim the entire selection. Glance through the selection quickly to see what other information you can pick up. Look for anything that will help you read fluently and with under-standing. Are there names, dates, or numbers? If so, you may have to read more slowly.

Reading for Meaning

Here are some ways to make sure you are making sense of what you read.

Build your concentration. You cannot understand what you read if you are not concentrating. When you discover that your thoughts are straying, correct the situation right away. Avoid distractions and distracting situations. Keep in mind the information you learned from previewing. This will help focus your attention on the selection.

Read in thought groups. Try to see meaningful combinations of words—phrases, clauses, or sentences. If you look at only one word at a time (called word-by-word reading), both your comprehension and your reading speed suffer.

Ask yourself questions. To sustain the pace you have set for yourself and to maintain a high level of concentration and comprehension, ask yourself questions such as What does this mean? or How can I use this information? as you read.

Finding the Main Ideas

The paragraph is the basic unit of meaning. If you can quickly discover and understand the main idea of each paragraph, you will build your comprehension of the selection.

Find the topic sentence. The topic sentence, which contains the main idea, often is the first sentence of a paragraph. It is followed by sentences that support, develop, or explain the main idea. Sometimes a topic sentence comes at the end of a paragraph. When it does, the supporting details come first, building the base for the topic sentence. Some paragraphs do not have a topic sentence; all of the sentences combine to create a meaningful idea.

Understand paragraph structure. Every well-written paragraph has a purpose. The purpose may be to inform, define, explain, or illustrate. The purpose should always relate to the main idea and expand on it. As you read each paragraph, see how the body of the paragraph tells you more about the main idea.

Relate ideas as you read. As you read the selection, notice how the writer puts together ideas. As you discover the relationship between the ideas, the main ideas come through quickly and clearly.

Mastering Reading Comprehension

Reading fast is not useful if you don't remember or understand what you read. The two exercises in Part A provide a check on how well you have understood the article.

Recalling Facts

These multiple-choice questions provide a quick check to see how well you recall important information from the article. As you learn to apply the reading strategies described earlier, you should be able to answer these questions more successfully.

Understanding Ideas

These questions require you to think about the main ideas in the article. Some main ideas are stated in the article; others are not. To answer some of the questions, you need to draw conclusions about what you read.

The five exercises in Part B require multiple answers. These exercises provide practice in applying comprehension and critical thinking skills that you can use in all your reading.

Recognizing Words in Context

Always check to see whether the words around an unfamiliar word—its context—can give you a clue to the word's meaning. A word generally appears in a context related to its meaning.

Suppose, for example, that you are unsure of the meaning of the word *expired* in the following passage:

> Vera wanted to check out a book, but her library card had expired. She had to borrow my card, because she didn't have time to renew hers.

You could begin to figure out the meaning of *expired* by asking yourself a question such as, What could have happened to Vera's library card that would make her need to borrow someone else's card? You might realize that if Vera had to renew her card, its usefulness must have come to an end or run out. This would lead you to conclude that the word *expired* must mean "to come to an end" or "to run out." You would be right. The context suggested the meaning.

Context can also affect the meaning of a word you already know. The word *key*, for instance, has many meanings. There are musical keys, door keys, and keys to solving a mystery. The context in which the word *key* occurs will tell you which meaning is correct.

Sometimes a word is explained by the words that immediately follow it. The subject of a sentence and your knowledge about that subject might also help you determine the meaning of an unknown word. Try to decide the meaning of the word *revive* in the following sentence:

> Sunshine and water will revive those drooping plants.

The compound subject is *sunshine* and *water*. You know that plants need light and water to survive and that drooping plants are not healthy. You can figure out that *revive* means "to bring back to health."

Distinguishing Fact from Opinion

Every day you are called upon to sort out fact and opinion. Because much of what you read and hear contains both facts and opinions, you need to be able to tell the two apart.

Facts are statements that can be proved. The proof must be objective and verifiable. You must be able to check for yourself to confirm a fact.

Look at the following facts. Notice that they can be checked for accuracy and confirmed. Suggested sources for verification appear in parentheses.

- Abraham Lincoln was the 16th president of the United States. (Consult biographies, social studies books, encyclopedias, and similar sources.)

- Earth revolves around the Sun. (Research in encyclopedias or astronomy books; ask knowledgeable people.)

- Dogs walk on four legs. (See for yourself.)

Opinions are statements that cannot be proved. There is no objective evidence you can consult to check the truthfulness of an opinion. Unlike facts, opinions express personal beliefs or judgments. Opinions reveal how someone feels about a subject, not the facts about that subject. You might agree or disagree with someone's opinion, but you cannot prove it right or wrong.

Look at the following opinions. The reasons these statements are classified as opinions appear in parentheses.

- Abraham Lincoln was born to be a president. (You cannot prove this by referring to birth records. There is no evidence to support this belief.)

- Earth is the only planet in our solar system where intelligent life exists. (There is no proof of this. It may be proved true some day, but for now it is just an educated guess—not a fact.)

- The dog is a human's best friend. (This is not a fact; your best friend might not be a dog.)

As you read, be aware that facts and opinions are often mixed together. Both are useful to you as a reader. But to evaluate what you read and to read intelligently, you need to know the difference between the two.

Keeping Events in Order

Sequence, or chronological order, is the order of events in a story or article or the order of steps in a process. Paying attention to the sequence of events or steps will help you follow what is happening, predict what might happen next, and make sense of a passage.

To make the sequence as clear as possible, writers often use signal words to help the reader get a more exact idea of when things happen. Following is a list of frequently used signal words and phrases:

until	first
next	then
before	after
finally	later
when	while
during	now
at the end	by the time
as soon as	in the beginning

Signal words and phrases are also useful when a writer chooses to relate details or events out of sequence. You need to pay careful attention to determine the correct chronological order.

Making Correct Inferences

Much of what you read *suggests* more than it *says*. Writers often do not state ideas directly in a text. They can't. Think of the time and space it would take to state every idea. And think of how boring that would be! Instead, writers leave it to you, the reader, to fill in the information they leave out—to make inferences. You do this by combining clues in the story or article with knowledge from your own experience.

You make many inferences every day. Suppose, for example, that you are visiting a friend's house for the first time. You see a bag of kitty litter. You infer (make an inference) that the family has a cat. Another day you overhear a conversation. You catch the names of two actors and the words *scene, dialogue,* and *directing.* You infer that the people are discussing a movie or play.

In these situations and others like them, you infer unstated information from what you observe or read. Readers must make inferences in order to understand text.

Be careful about the inferences you make. One set of facts may suggest several inferences. Some of these inferences could be faulty. A correct inference must be supported by evidence.

Remember that bag of kitty litter that caused you to infer that your friend has a cat? That could be a faulty inference. Perhaps your friend's family uses the kitty litter on their icy sidewalks to create traction. To be sure your inference is correct, you need more evidence.

Understanding Main Ideas

The main idea is the most important idea in a paragraph or passage—the idea that provides purpose and direction. The rest of the selection explains, develops, or supports the main idea. Without a main idea, there would be only a collection of unconnected thoughts.

In the following paragraph, the main idea is printed in italics. As you read, observe how the other sentences develop or explain the main idea.

Typhoon Chris hit with full fury today on the central coast of Japan. Heavy rain from the storm flooded the area. High waves carried many homes into the sea. People now fear that the heavy rains will cause mudslides in the central part of the country. The number of people killed by the storm may climb past the 200 mark by Saturday.

In this paragraph, the main-idea statement appears first. It is followed by sentences that explain, support, or give details. Sometimes the main idea appears at the end of a paragraph. Writers often put the main idea at the end of a paragraph when their purpose is to persuade or convince. Readers may be more open to a new idea if the reasons for it are presented first.

As you read the following paragraph, think about the overall impact of the supporting ideas. Their purpose is to convince the reader that the main idea in the last sentence should be accepted.

Last week there was a head-on collision at Huntington and Canton streets. Just a month ago a pedestrian was struck there. Fortunately, she was only slightly injured. In the past year, there have been more accidents there than at any other corner in the city. In fact, nearly 10 percent of all accidents in the city occur at the corner. This intersection is very dangerous, and a traffic signal should be installed there before a life is lost.

The details in the paragraph progress from least important to most important. They achieve their full effect in the main idea statement at the end.

In many cases, the main idea is not expressed in a single sentence. The reader is called upon to interpret all of the ideas expressed in the paragraph and to decide upon a main idea. Read the following paragraph.

> The American author Jack London was once a pupil at the Cole Grammar School in Oakland, California. Each morning the class sang a song. When the teacher noticed that Jack wouldn't sing, she sent him to the principal. He returned to class with a note. The note said that Jack could be excused from singing with the class if he would write an essay every morning.

In this paragraph, the reader has to interpret the individual ideas and to decide on a main idea. This main idea seems reasonable: Jack London's career as a writer began with a punishment in grammar school.

Understanding the concept of the main idea and knowing how to find it is important. Transferring that understanding to your reading and study is also important.

Working Through a Lesson

Part A

1. **Preview the article.** Locate the timed selection in Part A of the lesson that you are going to read. Wait for your teacher's signal to preview. You will have 20 seconds for previewing. Follow the previewing steps described on page 2.

2. **Read the article.** When your teacher gives you the signal, begin reading. Read carefully so that you will be able to answer questions about what you have read. When you finish reading, look at the board and note your reading time. Write this time at the bottom of the page on the line labeled Reading Time.

3. **Complete the exercises.** Answer the 10 questions that follow the article. There are 5 fact questions and 5 idea questions. Choose the best answer to each question and put an X in that box.

4. **Correct your work.** Use the Answer Key at the back of the book to check your answers. Circle any wrong answer and put an X in the box you should have marked. Record the number of correct answers on the appropriate line at the end of the lesson.

Part B

1. **Preview and read the passage.** Use the same techniques you

used to read Part A. Think about what you are reading.

2. **Complete the exercises.** Instructions are given for answering each category of question. There are 15 responses for you to record.

3. **Correct your work.** Use the Answer Key at the back of the book. Circle any wrong answer and write the correct letter or number next to it. Record the number of correct answers on the appropriate line at the end of the lesson.

Plotting Your Progress

1. **Find your reading rate.** Turn to the Reading Rate graph on page 116. Put an X at the point where the vertical line that represents the lesson intersects your reading time, shown along the left-hand side. The right-hand side of the graph will reveal your words-per-minute reading speed.

2. **Find your comprehension score.** Add your scores for Part A and Part B to determine your total number of correct answers. Turn to the Comprehension Score Graph on page 117. Put an X at the point where the vertical line that represents your lesson intersects your total correct answers, shown along the left-hand side. The right-hand side of the graph will show the percentage of questions you answered correctly.

3. **Complete the Comprehension Skills Profile.** Turn to page 118. Record your incorrect answers for the Part B exercises. The five Part B skills are listed along the bottom. There are five columns of boxes, one column for each question. For every incorrect answer, put an X in a box for that skill.

To get the most benefit from these lessons, you need to take charge of your own progress in improving your reading speed and comprehension. Studying these graphs will help you to see whether your reading rate is increasing and to determine what skills you need to work on. Your teacher will also review the graphs to check your progress.

TO THE TEACHER

About the Series

Timed Readings Plus in Social Studies includes 10 books at reading levels 4–13, with one book at each level. Book One contains material at a fourth-grade reading level; Book Two at a fifth-grade level, and so on. The readability level is determined by the Fry Readability Scale and is not to be confused with grade or age level of the student. The books are designed for use with students at middle school level and above.

The purposes of the series are as follows:

- to provide systematic, structured reading practice that helps students improve their reading rate and comprehension skills

- to give students practice in reading and understanding informational articles in the content area of social studies

- to give students experience in reading various text types—informational, expository, narrative, and prescriptive

- to prepare students for taking standardized tests that include timed reading passages in various content areas

- to provide materials with a wide range of reading levels so that students can continue to practice and improve their reading rate and comprehension skills

Because the books are designed for use with students at designated reading levels rather than in a particular grade, the social studies topics in this series are not correlated to any grade-level curriculum. Most standardized tests require students to read and comprehend social studies passages. This series provides an opportunity for students to become familiar with the particular requirements of reading social studies. For example, the vocabulary in a social studies article is important. Students need to know certain words in order to understand the concepts and the information.

Each book in the series contains 25 two-part lessons. Part A focuses on improving reading rate. This section of the lesson consists of a 400-word timed informational article on a social studies topic followed by two multiple-choice exercises. Recalling Facts includes five fact questions; Understanding Ideas includes five critical thinking questions.

Part B concentrates on building mastery in critical areas of comprehension. This section consists of a nontimed passage—the "plus" passage—followed by five exercises that address five major comprehension skills. The passage varies in length; its subject matter relates to the content of the timed selection.

Timed Reading and Comprehension

Timed reading is the best-known method of improving reading speed. There is no point in someone's reading at an accelerated speed if the person does not understand what she or he is reading. Nothing is more important than comprehension in reading. The main purpose of reading is to gain knowledge and insight, to understand the information that the writer and the text are communicating.

Few students will be able to read a passage once and answer all of the questions correctly. A score of 70 or 80 percent correct is normal. If the student gets 90 or 100 percent correct, he or she is either reading too slowly or the material is at too low a reading level. A comprehension or critical thinking score of less than 70 percent indicates a need for improvement.

One method of improving comprehension and critical thinking skills is for the student to go back and study each incorrect answer. First, the student should reread the question carefully. It is surprising how many students get the wrong answer simply because they have not read the question carefully. Then the student should look back in the passage to find the place where the question is answered, reread that part of the passage, and think about how to arrive at the correct answer. It is important to be able to recognize a correct answer when it is embedded in the text. Teacher guidance or class discussion will help the student find an answer.

Speed Versus Comprehension

It is not unusual for comprehension scores to decline as reading rate increases during the early weeks of timed readings. If this happens, students should attempt to level off their speed—but not lower it—and concentrate more on comprehension. Usually, if students maintain the higher speed and concentrate on comprehension, scores will gradually improve and within a week or two be back up to normal levels of 70 to 80 percent.

It is important to achieve a proper balance between speed and comprehension. An inefficient reader typically reads everything at one speed, usually slowly. Some poor readers, however, read rapidly but without satisfactory comprehension. It is important to achieve a balance between speed and comprehension. The practice that this series provides enables students to increase their reading speed while maintaining normal levels of comprehension.

Getting Started

As a rule, the passages in a book designed to improve reading speed should be relatively easy. The student should not have much difficulty with the vocabulary or the subject matter. Don't worry about the passages being too easy; students should see how quickly and efficiently they can read a passage.

Begin by assigning students to a level. A student should start with a book that is one level below his or her current reading level. If a student's reading level is not known, a suitable starting point would be one or two levels below the student's present grade in school.

Introduce students to the contents and format of the book they are using. Examine the book to see how it is organized. Talk about the parts of each lesson. Discuss the purpose of timed reading and the use of the progress graphs at the back of the book.

Timing the Reading

One suggestion for timing the reading is to have all students begin reading the selection at the same time. After one minute, write on the board the time that has elapsed and begin updating it at 10-second intervals (1:00, 1:10, 1:20, etc.). Another option is to have individual students time themselves with a stopwatch.

Teaching a Lesson

Part A

1. Give students the signal to begin previewing the lesson. Allow 20 seconds, then discuss special terms or vocabulary that students found.

2. Use one of the methods described above to time students as they read the passage. (Include the 20-second preview time as part of the first minute.) Tell students to write down the last time shown on the board or the stopwatch when they finish reading. Have them record the time in the designated space after the passage.

3. Next, have students complete the exercises in Part A. Work with them to check their answers, using the Answer Key that begins on page 114. Have them circle incorrect answers, mark the correct answers, and then record the numbers of correct answers for Part A on the appropriate line at the end of the lesson. Correct responses to eight or more questions indicate satisfactory comprehension and recall.

Part B

1. Have students read the Part B passage and complete the exercises that follow it. Directions are provided with each exercise. Correct responses require deliberation and discrimination.

2. Work with students to check their answers. Then discuss the answers with them and have them record the number of correct answers for Part B at the end of the lesson.

Have students study the correct answers to the questions they answered incorrectly. It is important that they understand why a particular answer is correct or incorrect.

Have them reread relevant parts of a passage to clarify an answer. An effective cooperative activity is to have students work in pairs to discuss their answers, explain why they chose the answers they did, and try to resolve differences.

Monitoring Progress

Have students find their total correct answers for the lesson and record their reading time and scores on the graphs on pages 116 and 117. Then have them complete the Comprehension Skills Profile on page 118. For each incorrect response to a question in Part B, students should mark an X in the box above each question type.

The legend on the Reading Rate graph automatically converts reading times to words-per-minute rates. The Comprehension Score graph automatically converts the raw scores to percentages.

These graphs provide a visual record of a student's progress. This record gives the student and you an opportunity to evaluate the student's progress and to determine the types of exercises and skills he or she needs to concentrate on.

Diagnosis and Evaluation

The following are typical reading rates.

Slow Reader—150 Words Per Minute

Average Reader—250 Words Per Minute

Fast Reader—350 Words Per Minute

A student who consistently reads at an average or above-average rate (with satisfactory comprehension) is ready to advance to the next book in the series.

A column of Xs in the Comprehension Skills Profile indicates a specific comprehension weakness. Using the profile, you can assess trends in student performance and suggest remedial work if necessary.

Early Images Create Myths of the West

In the nineteenth century, the United States grew quickly. Artists who explored the frontier produced an array of works depicting Western scenes. Some mass-produced their works; others displayed them in traveling shows. These artists offered the public some of the first views of the West. Their works shaped people's views of the Western frontier.

In large part, the works of these artists described the Western frontier of myth. Many of the artists depicted landscapes and cultures yet untouched by the modern world. In fact, settlement had already destroyed aspects of the natural environment and the way of life of many Native Americans. Some artists portrayed vast, unspoiled landscapes. Others portrayed Native Americans as noble savages in perfect harmony with nature.

The works of Albert Bierstadt and Thomas Moran are examples of paintings that shaped the Western landscape of myth. Bierstadt painted vast scenes of endless plains and mountain ranges. Moran portrayed the wild splendor of such sites as the Grand Canyon.

Landscape photographers also played a part in shaping the mythic West. The western expanse appeared silent, still, and timeless in photos. Some artists portrayed pristine landscapes. Others, such as Carleton Watkins, explored humankind's union with nature. Watkins's pictures of Yosemite had such an impact that President Abraham Lincoln placed limits on the region to protect it from misuse.

Many artists' depictions of Native Americans portrayed rich cultures as unaffected by Western expansion. These artists sought to preserve the customs of Native Americans. George Catlin was one of the first artists to document Native cultures. His paintings showed their vanishing way of life. Likewise, photographer Edward S. Curtis recorded the diverse cultures of the West in his North American Indian Project. Both artists presented Native cultures of a recent past instead of revealing the current challenges faced by Native peoples seeking to adapt to their changing world.

Unlike Catlin and Curtis who sought to preserve a record of Native cultures, Frederic Remington's works called on the settler to tame the Wild West and its peoples. His inventive works explored the tensions between the celebrated cowhand and the Native peoples. Remington's works glorified white settlement. His images assumed that the settlers' takeover of the land was justified. Remington perpetuated one of the most popular of the white settlers' myths of the West.

Reading Time _____

Recalling Facts

1. In the United States in the nineteenth century, explorers and settlers came across unknown peoples and landforms as they
   - ❏ a. explored the Atlantic coast.
   - ❏ b. moved eastward.
   - ❏ c. moved westward.

2. Some of the first views of the West were offered to the public
   - ❏ a. by artists.
   - ❏ b. by journalists.
   - ❏ c. by news anchors.

3. George Catlin and Edward S. Curtis sought to document
   - ❏ a. the lifestyle of the settler.
   - ❏ b. the customs of Native Americans.
   - ❏ c. pristine landscapes.

4. Frederic Remington's work
   - ❏ a. perpetuated the white settlers' most popular myths of the West.
   - ❏ b. attempted to preserve the Native cultures, just as Catlin's and Curtis's works had.
   - ❏ c. was the first to document Native cultures.

5. Many of the artists depicted landscapes and cultures
   - ❏ a. in ruin due to misuse or exploitation.
   - ❏ b. untouched by the modern world.
   - ❏ c. in the process of changing.

Understanding Ideas

6. One can conclude from the passage that early artists of the West depicted
   - ❏ a. accurate records of conditions on the frontier.
   - ❏ b. mythic images of the frontier.
   - ❏ c. imaginative scenes with no basis in reality.

7. Western artists showed landscapes that were
   - ❏ a. overpopulated.
   - ❏ b. fertile and settled.
   - ❏ c. vast, wild, and unspoiled.

8. From the passage, one can conclude that a shared theme in most early Western works was
   - ❏ a. the original state of nature and humankind.
   - ❏ b. the development of natural resources for industry.
   - ❏ c. the importance of farming to early settlers.

9. One can conclude from the passage that the works of Catlin and Curtis contributed to the myth of the unspoiled West by
   - ❏ a. illustrating only landscapes.
   - ❏ b. focusing on cowhands.
   - ❏ c. avoiding images of challenges that Native Americans faced in their changing worlds.

10. Compared with paintings, photographs
    - ❏ a. contributed equally to the creation of the mythic West.
    - ❏ b. provided a more realistic image of the West.
    - ❏ c. expressed more imaginative views of the West.

Catlin's Indian Gallery

In 1830 painter George Catlin set out on a six-year mission to document the life of the Native Americans of the Plains. On his journey, Catlin produced a record of the Native cultures that were threatened by the nation's westward growth. He hoped that his work might someday serve as a national archive of Native cultures.

On his tour of the West, Catlin visited about 40 groups. He painted more than 470 works. Many Native people trusted Catlin. They revealed to him the customs of their cultures. Catlin recorded what he had learned in his paintings and in detailed notes. He also collected cultural artifacts.

From these paintings and artifacts, Catlin compiled a collection that he called the Indian Gallery. He exhibited this body of work in the United States as well as abroad. He gave lectures on Native cultures and published his work in a series of volumes.

Despite these achievements, Catlin was not content. His goal to establish a national collection was thwarted time after time. Each time he appealed to Congress, the measure failed to pass. At a time of great tension between settlers and Native peoples, Catlin's support of Native Americans angered some members of Congress. Not until 1879, seven years after Catlin's death, did the Smithsonian Institution finally accept Catlin's Indian Gallery for exhibit.

1. Recognizing Words in Context

Find the word *thwarted* in the passage. One definition below is closest to the meaning of that word. One definition has the opposite or nearly the opposite meaning. The remaining definition has a completely different meaning. Label the definitions C for *closest*, O for *opposite or nearly opposite*, and D for *different*.

_____ a. praised

_____ b. blocked

_____ c. supported

2. Distinguishing Fact from Opinion

Two of the statements below present *facts*, which can be proved. The other statement is an *opinion*, which expresses someone's thoughts or beliefs. Label the statements F for *fact* and O for *opinion*.

_____ a. George Catlin painted the Native Americans of the Plains.

_____ b. The Smithsonian Institution accepted the Indian Gallery.

_____ c. Catlin's paintings are the most important records of Plains cultures.

3. Keeping Events in Order

Number the statements below 1, 2, and 3 to show the order in which the events took place.

_____ a. Catlin traveled for six years, painting the Native Americans of the Plains and their ways of life.

_____ b. Catlin's goal of having a national collection was achieved when the Smithsonian Institution accepted his work.

_____ c. Catlin exhibited his works in the United States and abroad.

4. Making Correct Inferences

Two of the statements below are correct *inferences*, or reasonable guesses. They are based on information in the passage. The other statement is an incorrect, or faulty, inference. Label the statements C for *correct* inference and F for *faulty* inference.

_____ a. Catlin's support of Native Americans almost cost him his career.

_____ b. Catlin sought not only to paint Native Americans of the Plains but also to learn about their cultures.

_____ c. With time the importance of Catlin's work was nationally recognized.

5. Understanding Main Ideas

One of the statements below expresses the main idea of the passage. One statement is too general, or too broad. The other explains only part of the passage; it is too narrow. Label the statements M for *main idea*, B for *too broad*, and N for *too narrow*.

_____ a. George Catlin called his collection the Indian Gallery.

_____ b. With his paintings, notes, and artifacts, George Catlin created a national archive of Plains cultures.

_____ c. Painters sometimes use their art to tell stories about events in history.

Correct Answers, Part A _____

Correct Answers, Part B _____

Total Correct Answers _____

The Conservation President

In 1901, following the assassination of President William McKinley, Vice President Theodore Roosevelt took the oath of office. Up to that time, the general public had believed that the United States had an endless supply of natural resources. It is true that some effort had been made to preserve the wilderness. For instance, Yellowstone Park, the first national park, had been set up in 1872. However, there was no consistent government policy.

During his nearly eight years in office, Roosevelt did more than any president before him to protect our natural resources. He added some 150 million acres to the national forests. (These acres are made up of five national parks, four wildlife refuges, and 51 bird reservations.) He pushed through the Reclamation Act of 1902. This Act called for irrigation to reclaim arid lands in the West. In 1907 he set up the Inland Waterways Commission. Its first act was to take an inventory, the first of its kind, of all the natural resources in the United States.

Several factors lay behind Roosevelt's conservation campaign. His own love of the outdoors was part of it. In his youth, he had been a cowboy and a rancher. In addition, by opposing lumber, mining, and grazing lobbyists, he continued his fight against the rich and powerful. He was committed to help the common man, not "to help the rich man make more profit for his company."

Three men played a large role in the success of Roosevelt's conservation campaign. They were Gifford Pinchot, F. H. Newell, and W. J. McGee. While Roosevelt was governor of New York (1898–1899), Pinchot and Newell had helped him to work out state conservation policies. As president, Roosevelt placed the conservation of natural resources in the hands of experts committed to working together. He made Pinchot, a forestry expert, head of the Bureau of Forestry (now the U.S. Forest Service). Newell, a hydraulics engineer, became director of the Geological Survey. McGee, a conservationist and scientist, helped shape policy. Before this, all was in the hands of battling clerks and bureaucrats who were often influenced by private interests.

Several national parks and monuments honor Roosevelt. For example, there is Theodore Roosevelt National Park in western North Dakota, which includes a ranch he ran in the 1800s. Also, Theodore Roosevelt's face is one of four giant carvings of U.S. presidents to adorn Mount Rushmore in South Dakota.

Reading Time _____

Recalling Facts

1. Theodore Roosevelt's first term as president was unusual in that he
   - ❑ a. was president for only six months.
   - ❑ b. became president after the elected president was assassinated.
   - ❑ c. ran successfully for a second term.

2. Among the factors that drove Roosevelt's conservationism were his
   - ❑ a. wealth and desire for power.
   - ❑ b. support of lumber and mining lobbyists.
   - ❑ c. love of the outdoors and his fight against the rich and powerful.

3. Roosevelt's appointments to the Bureau of Forestry and the Geological Survey differed from earlier appointments in that he chose
   - ❑ a. specialists in those resources.
   - ❑ b. special-interest groups.
   - ❑ c. family members.

4. Yellowstone Park has special significance because it was
   - ❑ a. the first national park that Roosevelt set up.
   - ❑ b. the first U.S. national park.
   - ❑ c. part of a coherent government policy.

5. Mount Rushmore
   - ❑ a. was the first wildlife refuge area in the United States.
   - ❑ b. was the first national park in the United States.
   - ❑ c. is a national memorial that honors U.S. presidents, including Theodore Roosevelt.

Understanding Ideas

6. The fact that Roosevelt was a conservationist before he became president can be inferred because he had
   - ❑ a. been a cowboy in his youth.
   - ❑ b. once run a ranch.
   - ❑ c. created a conservation policy while governor of New York.

7. When Roosevelt took office, most Americans probably were
   - ❑ a. interested in conservation.
   - ❑ b. not interested in conservation.
   - ❑ c. worried about natural resources.

8. Of the following actions taken by Roosevelt, the one that best reflects his attitude toward big business is the
   - ❑ a. appointing of experts rather than bureaucrats to manage resources.
   - ❑ b. addition of 150 million acres to the national forests.
   - ❑ c. setting up of the Inland Waterways Commission.

9. Irrigation was important to the Reclamation Act of 1902 because
   - ❑ a. Western land was rich in forests.
   - ❑ b. water was needed to make land in the West suitable for farming and ranching.
   - ❑ c. the Inland Waterways Commission had just been formed.

10. The phrase *the common man* probably refers to
    - ❑ a. any American who needs financial help from the government.
    - ❑ b. the average American who works hard to make a living.
    - ❑ c. every American, rich or poor.

Yosemite, a National Treasure

Covering 761,757 acres in central California, Yosemite has often turned admirers into defenders. In 1851, a troop of soldiers, the Mariposa Battalion, was sent to the region by the governor on a mission. The mission failed, but soldiers extolled the beauties of the place. People poured in. Soon, private enterprise was threatening to take over Yosemite. Senator John Conness of California moved quickly to put a bill before Congress. The bill called for the state to preserve Yosemite and nearby Mariposa Grove. In 1864 the land grant was approved. Although Yellowstone was to become the first national park (1872), this grant made Yosemite the nation's first wilderness preserve.

In 1868 a young Scottish-born naturalist, John Muir, visited Yosemite Valley. Muir was appalled to find the region being overgrazed. Muir wrote about the need for further conservation efforts. He found a friend in publisher Robert Underwood Johnson, and the two made their case to Congress. As a result, Yosemite National Park was established in 1890. Sixteen years later, the grant reverted to the Federal government.

In 1903 President Theodore Roosevelt joined Muir. They camped where the Mariposa Battalion had once camped. These two champions of nature spoke of the need to protect wonders such as Yosemite. America's national parks, after all, are its national treasures.

1. Recognizing Words in Context

Find the word *extolled* in the passage. One definition below is closest to the meaning of that word. One definition has the opposite or nearly the opposite meaning. The remaining definition has a completely different meaning. Label the definitions C for *closest*, O for *opposite or nearly opposite*, and D for *different*.

_____ a. praised

_____ b. rang

_____ c. criticized

2. Distinguishing Fact from Opinion

Two of the statements below present *facts*, which can be proved. The other statement is an *opinion*, which expresses someone's thoughts or beliefs. Label the statements F for *fact* and O for *opinion*.

_____ a. In 1868 a young Scottish-born naturalist visited Yosemite Valley.

_____ b. Yosemite National Park is the nation's most glorious park.

_____ c. Yosemite became the nation's first wilderness preserve.

3. Keeping Events in Order

Number the statements below 1, 2, and 3 to show the order in which the events took place.

_____ a. John Muir first visits Yosemite and then fights to protect it.

_____ b. Congress passes a bill authorizing the State of California to protect and preserve Yosemite Valley.

_____ c. President Theodore Roosevelt camps out in Yosemite.

4. Making Correct Inferences

Two of the statements below are correct *inferences*, or reasonable guesses. They are based on information in the passage. The other statement is an incorrect, or faulty, inference. Label the statements C for *correct* inference and F for *faulty* inference.

_____ a. The state of California did not fully live up to its mandate to protect and preserve Yosemite.

_____ b. Robert Underwood Johnson believed in conservationism.

_____ c. If the Mariposa Battalion had not been sent to Yosemite, the area would not have been preserved.

5. Understanding Main Ideas

One of the statements below expresses the main idea of the passage. One statement is too general, or too broad. The other explains only part of the passage; it is too narrow. Label the statements M for *main idea*, B for *too broad*, and N for *too narrow*.

_____ a. National parks are national treasures.

_____ b. Yosemite National Park was established around the original California land grant in 1890.

_____ c. Thanks to the vision of conservationists, the natural beauty of Yosemite has been preserved for posterity.

Correct Answers, Part A _____

Correct Answers, Part B _____

Total Correct Answers _____

The Important Role of Farming in the Northwest Today

The Northwest region of the United States boasts rich soil and a mild climate. This drew early settlers to the land to farm. The ample rivers of Washington, Oregon, and Idaho made farming possible even in the driest parts of those regions. For close to a century, farmers there have relied on dams to harness the water to irrigate crops. As a result, the states in the region have become some of the largest U.S. crop producers. Chief crops include apples and potatoes.

Once a mainstay of the region's early economy, farming retains a key role in the Northwest today. Idaho's farms grow beans, grains, sugar beets, and fruits. They also produce about one-third of all potatoes grown in the nation. Likewise, Washington farmers are the top growers of apples and sweet cherries. In Oregon, by contrast, the diversity of crops is what sets it apart. Farmers there grow all kinds of grains, nuts, fruits, berries, vegetables, and beans.

Moreover, farming in the Northwest supports the livelihood of a major portion of the region's population. Although the trend in other parts of the nation is toward corporate farming, family farms make up most of the farms in the Northwest. In Oregon and Washington, more than 90 percent of farms are family owned.

Farming is also a large employer in each state. One in 10 workers in Idaho is employed in agriculture. In Washington, agriculture provides the third most employment. For the most part, farm workers in the region are Latinos from Mexico. Some of the region's farm workers live in the Northwest throughout the year. Others migrate to the region during harvest. So many migrant workers flood the region at harvest time that a lack of housing often results. One source suggests that more than one-third of the workforce is made up of immigrants without work papers. Another sizeable portion of the workforce is children aged 1 to 19.

In addition to providing jobs, farming plays another key role in the region. It supplies the raw goods for one of the Northwest's leading industries—food processing. In Idaho, plant workers freeze or dehydrate close to half of all potatoes grown. In Washington, workers can fruits, vegetables, and soups. They make flour and meal, as well, from the state's many grains. Although farming is no longer the primary industry in the Northwest, it continues to play a crucial role in the economy of the region.

Reading Time _____

Recalling Facts

1. Early settlers came to the Northwest to farm because of the
   - ❏ a. rich soil and mild climate.
   - ❏ b. abundant mineral resources.
   - ❏ c. plentiful fish and wildlife.

2. In the Northwest today, farming
   - ❏ a. is the primary industry.
   - ❏ b. retains an important role.
   - ❏ c. is mostly a failing industry.

3. Two chief crops of the Northwest region are
   - ❏ a. corn and beans.
   - ❏ b. apples and potatoes.
   - ❏ c. walnuts and cranberries.

4. In the Northwest, most farms are owned by
   - ❏ a. migrant workers.
   - ❏ b. corporations.
   - ❏ c. families.

5. Farming supplies the raw goods for one of the Northwest's leading industries,
   - ❏ a. food processing.
   - ❏ b. electronics.
   - ❏ c. shipbuilding.

Understanding Ideas

6. One can conclude from the passage that the Northwest region is made up of the states of
   - ❏ a. California, Nevada, and Oregon.
   - ❏ b. Montana and Washington.
   - ❏ c. Washington, Oregon, and Idaho.

7. Food processing is a leader in Northwest industries because of the
   - ❏ a. lack of "high-tech" industries in the region.
   - ❏ b. success of farming in the region.
   - ❏ c. fishing industry.

8. One can conclude that a migrant farm worker is a worker who
   - ❏ a. is under age 19.
   - ❏ b. has a permanent job on a farm.
   - ❏ c. moves from place to place with the harvest.

9. Which of the following statements best summarizes the main idea?
   - ❏ a. Although the farming industry has changed, it continues to play an important role in the economy of the Northwest.
   - ❏ b. Beans, grains, and fruits are grown in the Northwest.
   - ❏ c. The farming industry has changed all over the United States in the last century.

10. One can conclude that farming benefits the Northwest by providing
    - ❏ a. a wide range of crops, many jobs, and raw goods for other industries.
    - ❏ b. alternatives to factory work.
    - ❏ c. the highest income of all industries in the region.

3 B   The Importance of the Apple Industry in Washington

The state of Washington produces more than half of the apples grown for fresh eating in the United States. The state is home to thousands of orchards. Most of them are found in the Yakima and Wenatchee valleys. The mild climate, plentiful sunlight, cool river water, and rich soil of the region are perfect for growing apples.

Of all agricultural industries in Washington, growing apples is the most lucrative. It provides both jobs for workers and opportunities for a number of related businesses. Year round, a large orchard may employ 300 or more people to maintain the trees. At the end of a season, workers prune the trees, trimming and thinning the branches. Once the growing season begins, these workers observe the growth of the apples. They remove malformed or damaged fruits to allow just the best apples to grow. At harvest, the apple industry employs tens of thousands of workers to handpick the fruit. Once the apples are picked, thousands of packing workers box the apples to be stored in cold warehouses. Storage brings business to another 125 companies around the state. Finally, the growers sell the apples and ship them to all 50 states and more than 40 countries.

1. **Recognizing Words in Context**

   Find the word *lucrative* in the passage. One definition below is closest to the meaning of that word. One definition has the opposite or nearly the opposite meaning. The remaining definition has a completely different meaning. Label the definitions C for *closest*, O for *opposite or nearly opposite*, and D for *different*.

   _____ a. profitable

   _____ b. failing

   _____ c. capable

2. **Distinguishing Fact from Opinion**

   Two of the statements below present *facts*, which can be proved. The other statement is an *opinion*, which expresses someone's thoughts or beliefs. Label the statements F for *fact* and O for *opinion*.

   _____ a. The apple industry provides jobs for workers and business in the area.

   _____ b. Tens of thousands of workers handpick the apples at harvest.

   _____ c. Washington produces the finest apples in the nation.

3. Keeping Events in Order

Number the statements below 1, 2, and 3 to show the order in which the events take place.

_____ a. Packing workers box the apples for storage until they are sold.

_____ b. At harvest, workers handpick the fruits.

_____ c. Workers remove malformed and damaged fruits to allow only the best to grow.

4. Making Correct Inferences

Two of the statements below are correct *inferences,* or reasonable guesses. They are based on information in the passage. The other statement is an incorrect, or faulty, inference. Label the statements C for *correct* inference and F for *faulty* inference.

_____ a. Growers in Washington sell their apples throughout the world.

_____ b. Apple pickers are some of the highest paid workers.

_____ c. Apples are picked and packed by hand, probably because they are easily damaged.

5. Understanding Main Ideas

One of the statements below expresses the main idea of the passage. One statement is too general, or too broad. The other explains only part of the passage; it is too narrow. Label the statements M for *main idea,* B for *too broad,* and N for *too narrow.*

_____ a. The apple industry in Washington employs thousands of workers.

_____ b. The apple industry in Washington plays a key role in the local economy by providing business and employment in agriculture, packing, storage, and shipping.

_____ c. Agriculture in Washington plays an important role in the economy of the nation.

Correct Answers, Part A _____

Correct Answers, Part B _____

Total Correct Answers _____

Native Storytelling and Mary Louise Defender Wilson

Storytelling is part of a rich oral tradition among Native Americans. Much more than just a pastime, storytelling plays a vital role in Native cultures. It is a powerful teaching tool. It imparts a nation's values, history, and way of life to its people. The older generation passes along its traditions and accumulated wisdom to the younger generation. Thus, the sharing of stories from one generation to the next preserves one's cultural heritage.

Although Native stories vary from culture to culture, common themes prevail. A chief theme in most stories is respect for all life. Tales about plants, animals, the land, and nature honor all life and explore human connections with the Earth. Another typical theme is the link to a person's past. Creation stories and tales of ancestors explore this theme.

One person who has devoted her life to storytelling is Mary Louise Defender Wilson. Wilson was born in 1930 on the Standing Rock Indian Reservation in Shields, North Dakota. She grew up hearing Dakotah and Hidatsa stories from her mother and grandparents. Wilson's mother told her stories of the plants and animals she saw while traveling to and from work. Herding sheep in the fields, her grandfather told her tales about the rocks, buttes, and streams of their homeland. Through these stories and those of her Hidatsa grandmother, Wilson learned the values, beliefs, history, and language of her culture.

Today Wilson shares what she has learned whenever she can. She hosts Native-language radio programs and records bilingual stories on CDs for all to hear. Storytelling has played a large role in her work as a teacher and as the director of a number of programs. For her, storytelling is a way of life.

Wilson believes that the stories she tells convey valuable lessons. They teach history and reveal the interconnection of all life forms. Many stories she shares tell about local sites. One story about a rock near Fort Ransom, North Dakota, is of a woman who turned herself to stone because of her love of nature. Another tells of a woman who lived with a family of coyotes on a local butte. Wilson also shares the tale of the creation of the Dakotah people near Greater Bear's Lodge, a butte in North Dakota. Each of the stories she tells imparts a respect for nature, others, and for one's homeland, culture, and history.

Reading Time _____

Recalling Facts

1. A rich oral tradition in Native American cultures is
   - ❏ a. beading.
   - ❏ b. storytelling.
   - ❏ c. weaving.

2. To preserve cultural heritage, Native stories are
   - ❏ a. carved in stone.
   - ❏ b. written in books.
   - ❏ c. told by one generation to the next.

3. A chief theme in most Native American stories is
   - ❏ a. respect for all life.
   - ❏ b. the importance of winning.
   - ❏ c. the need for education.

4. Mary Louise Defender Wilson grew up hearing Dakotah and Hidatsa stories
   - ❏ a. in school.
   - ❏ b. from her mother and her grandparents.
   - ❏ c. from other children.

5. From the stories Wilson heard while growing up, she learned
   - ❏ a. the values, history, and language of her culture.
   - ❏ b. how to be a good teacher.
   - ❏ c. the difference between fact and fiction.

Understanding Ideas

6. From the passage, one can conclude that storytelling
   - ❏ a. is an amusing pastime.
   - ❏ b. continues to be an important cultural tradition.
   - ❏ c. is a complex art form that is not easily understood.

7. A likely setting for a Native American story is
   - ❏ a. a large city.
   - ❏ b. a distant land.
   - ❏ c. a homeland site.

8. It is likely that Wilson tells stories about rocks, landforms, and animals
   - ❏ a. to teach Native languages.
   - ❏ b. to honor important people.
   - ❏ c. to impart to others a respect for nature.

9. From the passage, one can infer that Wilson believes that
   - ❏ a. Native language is an important aspect of Native storytelling.
   - ❏ b. English is the best language for Native storytelling.
   - ❏ c. Native stories should be shared only with other Native people.

10. Compared with the traditions of Native storytelling as a whole, Wilson's storytelling
    - ❏ a. deals less with human connections to nature.
    - ❏ b. focuses to a larger extent on preserving cultural heritage.
    - ❏ c. shares to an equal extent the main themes of storytelling.

The Storyteller: A New Folk Art Theme

Sculpted clay figures are an admired form of Native American folk art. A favored piece is *Storyteller*. This type of clay figure honors the native tradition of telling stories. It consists of figures of a number of children seated around or on a central figure.

Not long ago in Cochiti pueblo, New Mexico, Helen Cordero made the first *Storyteller*. When a man asked her to make a large seated figure with children, Cordero thought of her grandfather. She recalled how all of the children came running to hear him tell his tales. As with the well-known *Singing Mother* figures, Cordero fashioned a seated figure with an open mouth. Her *Storyteller*, however, differed in key ways. The *Singing Mother* was a female figure with one child. Cordero's figure was male, with a number of children clinging to him. The piece was an instant success.

Over the next few decades, Cordero expanded the motif. In one sculpture, a figure kneels in prayer with children climbing up his back. In another, children seated on a wide apron surround a Navajo figure telling tales. For the work *Children's Hour*, clay children sit grouped around a central figure.

Following Cordero's lead, other pueblo artists have designed original storytelling figures ranging from animals to spirits. Together, they have instituted a new theme in pueblo art.

1. **Recognizing Words in Context**

   Find the word *fashioned* in the passage. One definition below is closest to the meaning of that word. One definition has the opposite or nearly the opposite meaning. The remaining definition has a completely different meaning. Label the definitions C for *closest*, O for *opposite or nearly opposite*, and D for *different*.

   _____ a. destroyed

   _____ b. made

   _____ c. dressed

2. **Distinguishing Fact from Opinion**

   Two of the statements below present *facts*, which can be proved. The other statement is an *opinion*, which expresses someone's thoughts or beliefs. Label the statements F for *fact* and O for *opinion*.

   _____ a. Helen Cordero made the first *Storyteller* figure.

   _____ b. Cordero's *Storyteller* figures are worthy of great praise.

   _____ c. The *Storyteller* figurine honors the Native tradition of telling stories.

3. **Keeping Events in Order**

Number the statements below 1, 2, and 3 to show the order in which the events took place.

_____ a. Cordero adapts the *Singing Mother* figure and makes the *Storyteller.*

_____ b. The storyteller theme evolves to include figures ranging from animals to spirits.

_____ c. Pueblo artists make clay *Singing Mother* figures.

4. **Making Correct Inferences**

Two of the statements below are correct *inferences,* or reasonable guesses. They are based on information in the passage. The other statement is an incorrect, or faulty, inference. Label the statements C for *correct* inference and F for *faulty* inference.

_____ a. The open mouth of the *Storyteller* figure symbolizes speech.

_____ b. With time and the varied contributions of different artists, folk-art traditions evolve to take on new forms.

_____ c. Although later pueblo artists made storytellers, their designs lacked Cordero's creativity.

5. **Understanding Main Ideas**

One of the statements below expresses the main idea of the passage. One statement is too general, or too broad. The other explains only part of the passage; it is too narrow. Label the statements M for *main idea,* B for *too broad,* and N for *too narrow.*

_____ a. Honoring her grandfather and the Native art of storytelling, Cordero inspires a new tradition of creating clay figures.

_____ b. Storytelling plays a vital role in Native American cultures.

_____ c. Cordero's first *Storyteller* was a male figure surrounded by a large number of children.

Correct Answers, Part A _____

Correct Answers, Part B _____

Total Correct Answers _____

The Story of the U.S. Postal Service

As early as the seventeenth century, an informal postal system existed in the United States. People relied on messengers to carry letters from place to place. As delivery systems developed, local officials set up post routes and post offices. Within a decade after the nation had gained freedom from Great Britain, a couple of thousand miles of post routes and about 76 post offices were in use.

The growth of the nation's early postal system is largely a result of the work of Benjamin Franklin. Franklin served as a postmaster for decades before being named postmaster general. In the years during which he worked for the postal system, he increased the number of post routes. He also made service faster and more frequent. His labor laid the framework for what would become the U.S. Postal Service. Over the next century and a half, the postal system expanded to include those services that define the system in use today.

Throughout the nineteenth century, the nation grew with the move westward. The postal system used horseback, stagecoach, steamboat, and railroad to carry mail. Early post routes West stretched overland by stagecoach or over sea by steamship. Each of these services took weeks at best. The need for faster transport was of constant concern. To speed the process, William Russell designed a horse-relay network known as the Pony Express. It reduced overland mail-travel time from the last railroad line in the East to the West Coast to only 10 days.

The postal system was also open to fresh ideas to improve service. In the twentieth century, the postal system experimented with new forms of transport. Early tests proved that motor vehicles would be very useful. As a result, the postal system possessed the first government-owned motor vehicle service. About the same time, the postal service experimented with air service. It proved to be the fastest carrier means yet.

In addition to new forms of transport, the postal system sought new ways to process the mail. They began using a five-digit coding system called the ZIP code as well as "high-tech" machines to speed sorting. Machines in use today read addresses, affix barcodes, sort, and process the mail at rates of more than nine pieces per second. Combined with advances in transport, these measures enable the U.S. Postal Service to continue providing the efficient and reliable service it is known for.

Reading Time _____

Recalling Facts

1. At the start of the colonial era, the postal system was
   - ❏ a. efficient.
   - ❏ b. widespread.
   - ❏ c. informal.

2. The growth of the nation's early postal system is largely the result of the work of postmaster
   - ❏ a. Benjamin Franklin.
   - ❏ b. Henry Zip.
   - ❏ c. William Russell.

3. To speed overland mail delivery to the West Coast, one man designed a horse-relay network called
   - ❏ a. the Pony Express.
   - ❏ b. airmail.
   - ❏ c. parcel post.

4. In the twentieth century, the postal system experimented with new forms of transport, such as
   - ❏ a. horseback and railroad.
   - ❏ b. motor vehicles and air service.
   - ❏ c. stagecoach and steamboat.

5. To speed mail sorting in the twentieth century, the postal service began to use
   - ❏ a. stamps.
   - ❏ b. ZIP codes and "high-tech" machines.
   - ❏ c. trucks

Understanding Ideas

6. Compared with early postal systems in the colonies, the U.S. Postal Service is
   - ❏ a. more highly structured.
   - ❏ b. less efficient.
   - ❏ c. smaller in delivery area.

7. A letter sent from the East Coast to the West Coast in the nineteenth century most likely would *not* have been carried by
   - ❏ a. horseback.
   - ❏ b. railroad.
   - ❏ c. airplane.

8. From the passage, one can conclude that the postal system was eager to experiment with new forms of transport in the twentieth century
   - ❏ a. to cut costs.
   - ❏ b. to increase the speed of delivery.
   - ❏ c. to establish post routes to the West coast.

9. One can conclude from the passage that speedy mail service today relies on air service and
   - ❏ a. automated mail-processing machines.
   - ❏ b. an increasing number of employees.
   - ❏ c. the Pony Express.

10. One can conclude from the passage that, as it developed, the U.S. Postal Service strove to provide
    - ❏ a. the least expensive service possible.
    - ❏ b. the fewest number of routes possible.
    - ❏ c. the fastest, most efficient, and most reliable service possible.

The Impact of Online Communications on the Postal Service

Technology has changed the way people correspond in the modern age. A century ago, sending a letter across the country took weeks. Today, it may arrive in mere seconds with e-mail. In addition, the Internet allows users to pay bills and conduct business online. One research group predicts that marketers will soon send more than twice as many advertisements via e-mail as they do by bulk mail via the postal service.

Some wonder about the impact of these new communication tools on the postal system. They fear the U.S. Postal Service will lose business. But in a recent five-year period, both volume and revenues for the Postal Service increased. Reports do cite some declines, however. First-class mail service, the service used to send letters, has fallen. Although one might assume the decline to be the result of increased e-mail use, the decrease apparently began before the e-mail age.

Although the full impact of e-mail on the Postal Service is not yet known, the intent of the Postal Service is plain. The Postal Service now offers online services. There is also talk of assigning an e-mail address to each postal address and installing e-mail for public use in all post offices. Clearly, the U.S. Postal Service has embraced this new technology.

1. Recognizing Words in Context

Find the word *embraced* in the passage. One definition below is closest to the meaning of that word. One definition has the opposite or nearly the opposite meaning. The remaining definition has a completely different meaning. Label the definitions C for *closest*, O for *opposite or nearly opposite*, and D for *different*.

_____ a. squeezed

_____ b. accepted

_____ c. rejected

2. Distinguishing Fact from Opinion

Two of the statements below present *facts*, which can be proved. The other statement is an *opinion*, which expresses someone's thoughts or beliefs. Label the statements F for *fact* and O for *opinion*.

_____ a. E-mail will only improve the services of the postal system.

_____ b. Although volume and revenues are up, some services of the postal system have declined.

_____ c. The postal system now offers online services.

3. Keeping Events in Order

Number the statements below 1, 2, and 3 to show the order in which the events took place.

_____ a. It is predicted that the number of advertisements sent by marketers via e-mail will more than double the number sent by bulk mail via the postal service.

_____ b. First-class mail service begins to decline.

_____ c. More and more people correspond via e-mail.

4. Making Correct Inferences

Two of the statements below are correct *inferences,* or reasonable guesses. They are based on information in the passage. The other statement is an incorrect, or faulty, inference. Label the statements C for *correct* inference and F for *faulty* inference.

_____ a. E-mail has caused the Postal Service to lose some business.

_____ b. The Postal Service has harnessed the new technology to improve and expand services.

_____ c. Technology has changed the way people correspond with one another and how they conduct business.

5. Understanding Main Ideas

One of the statements below expresses the main idea of the passage. One statement is too general, or too broad. The other explains only part of the passage; it is too narrow. Label the statements M for *main idea,* B for *too broad,* and N for *too narrow.*

_____ a. New technology has the potential to create large-scale social change.

_____ b. The U.S. Postal Service embraces the new technology of online services.

_____ c. Although the full impact of e-mail on the Postal Service is not yet known, the postal system appears to find the new technology as useful as the public does.

Correct Answers, Part A _____

Correct Answers, Part B _____

Total Correct Answers _____

The History of the Indigenous Peoples of Puerto Rico

The cultural heritage of the people of Puerto Rico is diverse. Indigenous people, Spaniards, people of African descent, and immigrants from across the globe call the island nation home. For thousands of years, however, the only people who lived on the island were Native peoples from the surrounding region.

The first people to live in Puerto Rico arrived on the island several thousand years ago. Experts believe that they came from North or South America on crude rafts. They settled on the coasts and survived by fishing, hunting, and gathering wild foods.

About 2,000 years ago, a new group, called the Igneri, arrived. They lived near the city of Ponce on a site known today as the Tibes Indigenous Ceremonial Center. In a dig at the site, experts found clay works made by this group.

At the same site, experts found proof of later residents. They were the Arawak and the Taino, a subgroup of the Arawak. The Arawak built ball courts and plazas of stone at the site. Because of their ability to build such structures, they are believed by experts to have had a highly ordered society made up of both leaders and workers. Experts have also found that the Arawak aligned some of the plazas with the movements of the sun, an arrangement that shows how vital the seasons were to their way of life as farmers.

The Taino began to inhabit the island of Puerto Rico about a thousand years ago. Unlike prior groups, they settled inland as well as along the coast. Some were hunters, farmers, and fishermen. Others were navigators, sailors, traders, and engineers. Their social structure was made up of a chief, priests, nobles, and a working class. Other central aspects of their culture were ball games, the arts, and religion.

The Taino flourished on the island for hundreds of years despite great challenges. The Caribs, a warlike group in the region, often raided the island for slaves. In the first part of the sixteenth century, Spaniards settled on the island, enslaving the Taino as well. Within a short time, most Taino had died from disease or overwork. The few who survived fled to the central mountains of the island. Today members of the Jatibonicu Taino Tribal Nation still live in these mountains. Although few Taino are left today, remnants of the culture—such as vocabulary, deities, musical instruments, and household items—are found throughout Puerto Rico.

Reading Time _____

Recalling Facts

1. For thousands of years, the only people who lived on the island of Puerto Rico were
   - ❑ a. Native peoples of the Americas.
   - ❑ b. African Americans.
   - ❑ c. Spaniards.

2. The first people to live in Puerto Rico settled on the coasts and survived by
   - ❑ a. fishing, hunting, and gathering wild foods.
   - ❑ b. trading goods with distant peoples.
   - ❑ c. running large plantations.

3. At the site known as Tibes Indigenous Ceremonial Center, the Arawak built
   - ❑ a. cliff dwellings.
   - ❑ b. giant pyramids.
   - ❑ c. ball courts and plazas.

4. On the island of Puerto Rico, Caribs and Spaniards enslaved
   - ❑ a. the Igneri people.
   - ❑ b. the Taino people.
   - ❑ c. the earliest inhabitants.

5. Vocabulary, deities, musical instruments, and household items found today throughout the island are remnants of
   - ❑ a. Carib culture.
   - ❑ b. Taino culture.
   - ❑ c. Igneri culture.

Understanding Ideas

6. From the passage, one can conclude that the most recent indigenous inhabitants of Puerto Rico are
   - ❑ a. the Igneri.
   - ❑ b. the Carib.
   - ❑ c. the Taino.

7. One can conclude from the passage that the Taino almost died out in the sixteenth century as a result of
   - ❑ a. enslavement, mistreatment, and disease.
   - ❑ b. a violent hurricane.
   - ❑ c. a civil war.

8. Compared with prior Igneri inhabitants, the early Taino had
   - ❑ a. a less structured social order.
   - ❑ b. a more highly developed society.
   - ❑ c. a greater dependence on the land.

9. Given their social structure, sports, and other customs, it is likely that the Taino were most closely related to
   - ❑ a. Spaniards.
   - ❑ b. African Americans.
   - ❑ c. the Arawak.

10. It is likely that the current knowledge of the early Igneri, Arawak, and Taino cultures was obtained from
    - ❑ a. documents written by natives from the era.
    - ❑ b. ancient storytellers.
    - ❑ c. experts' studies, such as those at Tibes.

A Visit to Caguana Indian Ceremonial Park

Miguel pulled into the lot at the Caguana Indian Ceremonial Park. After driving for nearly two hours into the central mountains of Puerto Rico from his hotel in San Juan, he had finally arrived at the sacred Taino site.

The first formations Miguel observed as he entered the park were 10 rectangular ball courts, called *bateyes*. These were demarcated by a border of small stones. Large stone monoliths having elaborate carvings depicting Taino myths marked out the sides of some of the courts as well. Miguel saw a large birdlike form and a woman in a headdress with froglike legs. Some of the stone carvings were so faint that he could not make them out.

Miguel imagined a ball game in progress hundreds of years ago. Perhaps as many as 60 players had been on the court at one time. Each player would have worn a stone ring around his or her waist. This ring was used for batting the rubber ball. Miguel imagined himself scoring a goal and then, despite his greatest efforts, losing points as the ball dropped to the ground.

Miguel walked to the center of the court, admiring the beautiful limestone hills all around him. He listened to the waters of the scenic Tanamá River one last time before turning to leave.

1. Recognizing Words in Context

Find the word *demarcated* in the passage. One definition below is closest to the meaning of that word. One definition has the opposite or nearly the opposite meaning. The remaining definition has a completely different meaning. Label the definitions C for *closest*, O for *opposite or nearly opposite,* and D for *different*.

_____ a. unbounded

_____ b. engineered

_____ c. outlined

2. Distinguishing Fact from Opinion

Two of the statements below present *facts,* which can be proved. The other statement is an *opinion,* which expresses someone's thoughts or beliefs. Label the statements F for *fact* and O for *opinion.*

_____ a. Caguana Indian Ceremonial Park is located in Puerto Rico.

_____ b. In early Taino culture, people played ball on special courts.

_____ c. The most interesting feature of Taino culture is the stone carvings.

3. **Keeping Events in Order**

Number the statements below 1, 2, and 3 to show the order in which the events took place.

_____ a. Miguel drives from San Juan through the central mountains of Puerto Rico.

_____ b. Taino workers place stones in a large rectangle to outline the court they will use for playing ball.

_____ c. Miguel observes remnants of early Taino cultures such as ball courts and petroglyphs.

4. **Making Correct Inferences**

Two of the statements below are correct *inferences*, or reasonable guesses. They are based on information in the passage. The other statement is an incorrect, or faulty, inference. Label the statements C for *correct* inference and F for *faulty* inference.

_____ a. The park at Caguana was a spiritual center as well as a sporting center.

_____ b. Taino descendants still use the ball courts regularly.

_____ c. Miguel is a tourist enjoying one of Puerto Rico's cultural sites.

5. **Understanding Main Ideas**

One of the statements below expresses the main idea of the passage. One statement is too general, or too broad. The other explains only part of the passage; it is too narrow. Label the statements M for *main idea*, B for *too broad*, and N for *too narrow*.

_____ a. Puerto Rico has a rich indigenous history.

_____ b. Taino Ruins at Caguana Indian Ceremonial Park can inform visitors and inspire them to imagine ancient times.

_____ c. In a Taino ball game, players earned points by scoring goals.

Correct Answers, Part A _____

Correct Answers, Part B _____

Total Correct Answers _____

The graduation ceremony marks a student's journey from one stage of life to the next. This ritual allows students to bid farewell to their schools and classes and to begin to imagine their futures. In this sense, it is a rite of passage.

Graduation observances throughout the world are performed in diverse ways. In some cultures, a graduation is a festive event in which parties play a more important role than ceremonies do. In other cultures, it is a solemn affair steeped in centuries of tradition. Common to all is a set of customs that characterizes graduation.

In many places, the ceremonial rite itself is rich with tradition. At universities in the United States and England, the event begins with a procession. Music is played, and professors carry banners and wear hoods of different colors to represent their fields of study. Next, the graduates file in and take their seats. The main part of the ceremony includes speeches and the awarding of diplomas. As graduates receive their diplomas, they flip the tassels on their hats from one side to the other.

Dress is another ritual aspect of graduation. In many cultures, graduates wear caps and gowns. In the United States and England, those receiving advanced degrees may wear hoods as well. The color and size of the hood denote the graduate's field of study and degree. The shape of the gown's sleeves also shows the degree level. In Finland graduates earning the highest degrees wear suits and special hats bearing their school emblem. In addition, men wear a velvet ribbon attached to their jackets, and women wear a velvet brooch. At the master's degree level in Finland, graduates wear laurel garlands woven by community members. On the other hand, some graduation attire is quite simple. In Hong Kong, graduates simply wear their school uniforms.

In a few cultures, festivities to celebrate graduation are more important than the ceremonies. In junior high school in Mexico, the dance party for graduates, teachers, friends, and family is the central event. In Norway high school seniors celebrate by playing pranks for weeks before their modest ceremony on the last day of school. For each prank carried out, students are given tokens to attach to their hats. One prank is to wake up teachers by blowing car horns early in the morning outside their homes. Each of these varied traditions marks an important passage in a student's life.

Reading Time _____

Recalling Facts

1. A ceremony to mark a student's passage from one stage of life to the next is
   - ❏ a. a birthday.
   - ❏ b. a graduation.
   - ❏ c. retirement.

2. Graduation may be a solemn affair steeped in tradition or
   - ❏ a. a special meal.
   - ❏ b. a mandatory exam.
   - ❏ c. a festive event or a party.

3. In the United States and England, the color and size of the hood often represent
   - ❏ a. the graduate's field of study and degree.
   - ❏ b. the university giving the degree.
   - ❏ c. the graduate's choice.

4. For the graduation ceremony in Hong Kong, graduates wear
   - ❏ a. caps, gowns, and hoods.
   - ❏ b. special hats, ribbons, and brooches.
   - ❏ c. school uniforms.

5. In Mexico, where junior high school graduates celebrate with dances, the festivities are
   - ❏ a. more important than the ceremonies.
   - ❏ b. a minor part of graduation.
   - ❏ c. discouraged by adults.

Understanding Ideas

6. From the passage, one can conclude that ritual aspects of graduations include
   - ❏ a. special food and drinks.
   - ❏ b. ceremonies, special attire, and celebrations.
   - ❏ c. final exams and speeches.

7. One can conclude from the passage that the purpose of graduation is
   - ❏ a. to initiate students into the next grade.
   - ❏ b. to test students' knowledge.
   - ❏ c. to celebrate the graduates' current accomplishments and embrace their future potential.

8. Compared with the pranks typical of graduates in Norway, the graduation customs in the United States and England are
   - ❏ a. less traditional.
   - ❏ b. more subdued.
   - ❏ c. more festive.

9. It is likely that a student dressed in a gown with bell-shaped sleeves and a wide hood lined with purple velvet is a graduate in
   - ❏ a. England.
   - ❏ b. Norway.
   - ❏ c. Hong Kong.

10. It is likely that flipping the tassel of the cap from one side to the other upon receiving the diploma signifies
    - ❏ a. the completion of the student's learning.
    - ❏ b. the graduate's passage from one stage of life to the next.
    - ❏ c. the importance of the graduation procession.

7   B   The Great Transformation

In Japan an important event in every child's life is the kindergarten graduation. Known as the "great transformation," this rite marks a child's passage from playful youngster to serious student.

Kindergarten in Japan is a time for children to learn through play. This style of active learning cultivates their minds and bodies. Teachers design programs that foster social skills, the use of language, the expression of thoughts and feelings, and an awareness of the natural world. Teachers also help to prepare children for the next level of study. Although children have a great deal of playtime in kindergarten, they learn to settle down quickly and focus when it is time for a lesson.

The great transformation signifies this passage in the youngster's life. The children conduct themselves with decorum during this formal event. They march into the room in single file with their arms held against their sides. When they reach the row of chairs in the center of the room, they take a bow all together. They then sit down silently. A number of adults give short speeches, and then the dean awards each student a certificate. After the children recite a farewell speech or sing a song, the ceremony closes. The seriousness of the great transformation helps to prepare children for the intense learning that lies ahead.

1. **Recognizing Words in Context**

   Find the word *cultivates* in the passage. One definition below is closest to the meaning of that word. One definition has the opposite or nearly the opposite meaning. The remaining definition has a completely different meaning. Label the definitions C for *closest*, O for *opposite or nearly opposite*, and D for *different*.

   _____ a. improves

   _____ b. weakens

   _____ c. characterizes

2. **Distinguishing Fact from Opinion**

   Two of the statements below present *facts*, which can be proved. The other statement is an *opinion*, which expresses someone's thoughts or beliefs. Label the statements F for *fact* and O for *opinion*.

   _____ a. In Japan, kindergarten graduation is called the great transformation.

   _____ b. Kindergarten is a great time in a child's life.

   _____ c. In kindergarten in Japan, children learn through play.

3. Keeping Events in Order

Number the statements below 1, 2, and 3 to show the order in which the events take place.

_____ a. The youngsters march into the room in single file and take a bow in unison.

_____ b. The children recite a farewell speech or sing a song.

_____ c. The dean awards each student a graduation certificate.

4. Making Correct Inferences

Two of the statements below are correct *inferences,* or reasonable guesses. They are based on information in the passage. The other statement is an incorrect, or faulty, inference. Label the statements C for *correct* inference and F for *faulty* inference.

_____ a. Because there is so much playtime, little learning occurs in kindergarten.

_____ b. In Japan, after kindergarten, school study is rigorous.

_____ c. The Japanese believe that physical self-control is essential to being a good student.

5. Understanding Main Ideas

One of the statements below expresses the main idea of the passage. One statement is too general, or too broad. The other explains only part of the passage; it is too narrow. Label the statements M for *main idea,* B for *too broad,* and N for *too narrow.*

_____ a. A rite of passage marks one's journey from one stage of life to the next.

_____ b. Kindergarten in Japan is a time for children to learn through play.

_____ c. The great transformation marks a child's passage from playful kindergarten student to serious student.

Correct Answers, Part A _____

Correct Answers, Part B _____

Total Correct Answers _____

The California Gold Rush

In 1848 carpenter James W. Marshall found gold at Sutter's Mill in California. He made his find while digging a canal for John Sutter's sawmill. At first, he and Sutter were able to keep the discovery a secret. Within a year, however, the news of this and other strikes spread across the United States and throughout the world.

At first people thought that the gold strikes in California were a fantastic tale. In San Francisco, a man named Sam Brannan marched up and down the streets, spreading the news of the strike. He carried a bottle filled with gold dust to convince the locals that the tale was true. For the rest of the nation, though, it took the words of President James Polk to confirm the news as fact.

As soon as people realized the tales were true, they became obsessed with "gold fever." Tens of thousands of people left their homes and headed for California. Some came from as far away as China, Chile, and Europe. In the United States, merchants closed their shops, farmers fled their fields, soldiers abandoned their posts, and doctors and lawyers forfeited their practices to fulfill dreams of instant wealth.

The harsh realities of the gold rush, however, quickly dashed the hopes of many newcomers. The journey required months of travel across hazardous lands or aboard crowded ships. Disease and other dangers claimed many lives. Once in California, the prospectors set up makeshift camps in the wilderness. They suffered from food shortages and also faced exposure to the elements, poor sanitation, illness, and isolation. Boomtowns developed in some regions to offer meals, boarding, and other services to miners. Although these shanty towns offered some benefits, crime was rampant. No matter where prospectors lived, the work they did was backbreaking. Panning for gold required the miners to stand in cold water for up to 10 hours a day digging, sifting, and washing the river sediment.

Within a matter of years, the gold became scarce. Very few struck it rich panning for gold in the California hills. However, the Gold Rush brought great fortune to businesses and to California as a whole. Before the Gold Rush, San Francisco had been a small port town with a few hundred residents. It grew to become a bustling city. Similarly, many mining camps became permanent townships. These aided in the settlement of the Western frontier.

Reading Time _____

Recalling Facts

1. In January 1948, James W. Marshall found gold at Sutter's Mill in
   - ❏ a. Alaska.
   - ❏ b. California.
   - ❏ c. Texas.

2. At first people thought that the gold strike in 1848 was
   - ❏ a. a fact rather than a rumor.
   - ❏ b. a trick to lure settlers to the West.
   - ❏ c. a fantastic tale.

3. The dream of those who hurried to California during the Gold Rush was
   - ❏ a. to obtain instant wealth.
   - ❏ b. to establish fertile farms.
   - ❏ c. to settle the frontier.

4. The journey to California during the Gold Rush required
   - ❏ a. unreliable railway transport.
   - ❏ b. expensive airline tickets.
   - ❏ c. months of travel overland or aboard ships.

5. The Gold Rush led to the growth of
   - ❏ a. San Francisco and new townships in California.
   - ❏ b. many miners' finding instant wealth.
   - ❏ c. public health regulations in the mining towns.

Understanding Ideas

6. One can conclude from the passage that people who had "gold fever"
   - ❏ a. suffered from chills and headaches.
   - ❏ b. left home and all commitments, hoping to strike it rich in California.
   - ❏ c. lost their minds after acquiring instant wealth.

7. Compared with the dreams of the gold miners, the realities of the Gold Rush offered
   - ❏ a. greater prospects of wealth.
   - ❏ b. less comfortable living conditions.
   - ❏ c. fewer jobs.

8. Prospectors in the California Gold Rush were likely to be people who
   - ❏ a. were not afraid to take risks.
   - ❏ b. required modern comforts.
   - ❏ c. strongly disliked adventure.

9. From the passage, one can conclude that the Gold Rush not only aided the settlement of California but also
   - ❏ a. fulfilled the dreams of all prospectors.
   - ❏ b. improved education systems.
   - ❏ c. fueled the growth of business and commerce.

10. A business entrepreneur unlikely to succeed in a mining camp would have been a
   - ❏ a. skilled cook.
   - ❏ b. mining-tool supplier.
   - ❏ c. fine-furniture dealer.

What Are Ghost Towns?

Ghost towns are the sites of former municipalities that have been abandoned by their inhabitants. Most were once farming communities or bustling centers of commerce, but when the cattle drives ended, crops failed, or ore became scarce, the inhabitants of the towns moved away. Many of the structures they left behind a century ago still stand today. These buildings offer a rare glimpse into the nation's past.

Most of the ghost towns found in the United States are in the West. Many were once mining camps. When miners settled in an area, they needed the services of merchants, bankers, and other entrepreneurs. A hotel, a boarding house, a saloon, and a general store were businesses found in almost every town.

Just as merchants and entrepreneurs followed miners to towns, they also left when the miners moved on. When ore grew scarce, miners no longer had a way to make a living and had no choice but to seek their fortunes elsewhere. As a result, the businesses failed, and the remaining inhabitants forsook the dying town.

In some ghost towns, buildings stand intact; in others, time and weather have reduced the structures to earthen mounds or scattered debris. In either case, the ruins offer a sense of the nation's history and the passage of time.

1. Recognizing Words in Context

Find the word *forsook* in the passage. One definition below is closest to the meaning of that word. One definition has the opposite or nearly the opposite meaning. The remaining definition has a completely different meaning. Label the definitions C for *closest*, O for *opposite or nearly opposite*, and D for *different*.

_____ a. deserted

_____ b. took out

_____ c. remained in

2. Distinguishing Fact from Opinion

Two of the statements below present *facts*, which can be proved. The other statement is an *opinion*, which expresses someone's thoughts or beliefs. Label the statements F for *fact* and O for *opinion*.

_____ a. Ghost towns are haunting reminders of the nation's past.

_____ b. When miners abandoned towns, local businesses failed.

_____ c. Ghost towns are towns abandoned by their inhabitants.

3. Keeping Events in Order

Number the statements below 1, 2, and 3 to show the order in which the events took place.

———— a. When ore grew scarce, miners and business owners abandoned the area.

———— b. Merchants and entrepreneurs established businesses in mining towns.

———— c. Miners settled in an area rich in ore.

4. Making Correct Inferences

Two of the statements below are correct *inferences,* or reasonable guesses. They are based on information in the passage. The other statement is an incorrect, or faulty, inference. Label the statements C for *correct* inference and F for *faulty* inference.

———— a. Ghost towns contain evidence of former inhabitants.

———— b. A town fails if inhabitants have no way to make a living.

———— c. Every ghost town had been a former mining town.

5. Understanding Main Ideas

One of the statements below expresses the main idea of the passage. One statement is too general, or too broad. The other explains only part of the passage; it is too narrow. Label the statements M for *main idea,* B for *too broad,* and N for *too narrow.*

———— a. The sites of ruins offer historical evidence that provides insight into the past.

———— b. Ghost towns still standing today were created when residents no longer could earn a living and left.

———— c. In each mining town, a hotel, a boarding house, a saloon, and a general store were found.

Correct Answers, Part A ————

Correct Answers, Part B ————

Total Correct Answers ————

Diverse Forms of Martial Arts

Martial arts take many forms. There are combat sports, self-defense techniques, performing arts, and styles of meditation. They improve fitness as well as mental focus. Over thousands of years, early forms of martial arts spread from monks to warriors to everyday people.

Today people practice martial arts all over the world. In India martial artists practice an ancient form of combat called *kalaripayit*. It involves kicks, punches, strikes, throws, and holds. Hundreds of years ago in Brazil, enslaved Africans developed a martial art called *capoeira*. This dancelike form involves kicks, takedowns, and acrobatic movements. Tae kwon do, the national sport of Korea, is also an Olympic sport. This martial art resembles karate but incorporates more kicks.

Perhaps the best known of the martial arts are forms from China and Japan. People the world over practice the diverse martial arts traditions of these two cultures. In China hundreds of forms of martial arts exist. One of the oldest and most practiced styles is kung fu. Shaolin monks first developed it thousands of years ago to defend themselves from thieves. From stances named for animals, a kung fu martial artist exerts strikes, punches, and kicks while deflecting an opponent's blows with blocks. Students who practice kung fu or other martial arts as combat sports do so by sparring. When students spar, they do not use full force with strikes in order not to hurt one another.

Many forms of Chinese martial arts, including some forms of kung fu, are not used for combat. Wu shu is a dancelike martial art and competitive sport. Those who practice forms of wu shu use combat routines and weapons, but the focus is on grace, flexibility, and coordination. Some even practice wu shu to music. Likewise, students of t'ai chi do not practice the art as a combat sport but, rather, as a form of movement to promote well-being.

The martial arts of Japan are similarly diverse. Karate, jujitsu, judo, and aikido are some of the best-known forms. Although karate and jujitsu are both combat sports, the techniques of these two martial arts differ greatly. In contrast to karate, which, like kung fu, uses punches, strikes, kicks, and blocks, jujitsu uses grappling techniques. Like wrestling, grappling involves a variety of throws and holds. Judo and aikido use grappling techniques also, but they are much less combative forms than jujitsu. These meditative forms teach grappling methods to be used only in self-defense.

Reading Time _____

Recalling Facts

1. In addition to being combat sports, martial arts are also
   - ❏ a. self-defense techniques, performing arts, and styles of meditation.
   - ❏ b. forms of modern-day warfare.
   - ❏ c. methods of hunting.

2. Enslaved Africans developed a dance-like martial art called capoeira in
   - ❏ a. China.
   - ❏ b. Japan.
   - ❏ c. Brazil.

3. One of the oldest and most practiced Chinese martial arts is
   - ❏ a. judo.
   - ❏ b. kung fu.
   - ❏ c. jujitsu.

4. To avoid hurting one another, students who practice martial arts as combat sports
   - ❏ a. spar.
   - ❏ b. do not touch one another.
   - ❏ c. wrestle.

5. Karate uses punches, strikes, and kicks—in contrast to jujitsu, judo, and aikido, which use
   - ❏ a. dance movements.
   - ❏ b. boxing techniques.
   - ❏ c. grappling or wrestling techniques.

Understanding Ideas

6. From the passage, one can infer that martial arts have origins in
   - ❏ a. warfare.
   - ❏ b. diverse cultures and traditions.
   - ❏ c. Chinese traditions.

7. One can conclude from the passage that all martial arts styles involve
   - ❏ a. movement.
   - ❏ b. combat.
   - ❏ c. meditation.

8. Compared with the martial art t'ai chi, which promotes health, karate is
   - ❏ a. older.
   - ❏ b. less physical.
   - ❏ ç. more combative.

9. It is likely that students practice martial arts today
   - ❏ a. to prepare for war.
   - ❏ b. to gain fitness and mental focus and to learn self-defense techniques.
   - ❏ c. to become better dancers.

10. Which of the following statements best describes the main idea of the passage?
    - ❏ a. Combat styles of martial arts involve kicks, punches, strikes, throws, and holds.
    - ❏ b. Rigorous physical activity, such as practicing one of the martial arts, can lead to a healthier life.
    - ❏ c. The origins, practices, and purpose of martial arts vary greatly from one tradition to another.

The Triumph of Capoeira

Capoeira, a Brazilian martial art, is a game performed to music. It involves aspects of dance, play, combat, and ritual. With just the hands, feet, or head touching the ground, the players move from stance to stance like acrobats. One player performs a strike. The other gracefully retreats by swaying under or around the blow.

Enslaved Africans in Brazil first created capoeira hundreds of years ago. They combined African dance and ritual customs with new art forms developed in Brazil. Because fighting was banned, they tried to disguise the martial art as an innocuous dance. However, slaveholders were still threatened by the power of the game. They banned the game and cruelly punished any players they caught engaging in it.

Even after the government freed the enslaved Africans, there was a ban on capoeira. In fact, one president signed an act to outlaw the martial art. As they had for hundreds of years, African Brazilians continued to play the game in secret.

Finally, a few decades later, officials lifted the ban. One master called Mestre Bimba opened the first capoeira school in 1932. Even without the ban, officials required the first schools to register with the police. Despite these obstacles, capoeira has become a national sport in Brazil. Today players practice capoeira throughout the world.

1. Recognizing Words in Context

Find the word *innocuous* in the passage. One definition below is closest to the meaning of that word. One definition has the opposite or nearly the opposite meaning. The remaining definition has a completely different meaning. Label the definitions C for *closest*, O for *opposite or nearly opposite*, and D for *different*.

_____ a. harmless

_____ b. offensive

_____ c. clumsy

2. Distinguishing Fact from Opinion

Two of the statements below present *facts*, which can be proved. The other statement is an *opinion*, which expresses someone's thoughts or beliefs. Label the statements F for *fact* and O for *opinion*.

_____ a. Enslaved Africans in Brazil created capoeira.

_____ b. Officials in Brazil once banned capoeira.

_____ c. Capoeira is one of the most graceful martial arts.

3. **Keeping Events in Order**

   Number the statements below 1, 2, and 3 to show the order in which the events took place.

   _____ a. The government lifts the ban against capoeira.

   _____ b. Officials require the first capoeira schools to register with police.

   _____ c. Capoeira is named a national sport in Brazil.

4. **Making Correct Inferences**

   Two of the statements below are correct *inferences*, or reasonable guesses. They are based on information in the passage. The other statement is an incorrect, or faulty, inference. Label the statements C for *correct* inference and F for *faulty* inference.

   _____ a. Over time capoeira gained favor in Brazil.

   _____ b. Enslaved Africans based capoeira on ancient African martial arts.

   _____ c. Capoeira is as much a performing art as it is a martial art.

5. **Understanding Main Ideas**

   One of the statements below expresses the main idea of the passage. One statement is too general, or too broad. The other explains only part of the passage; it is too narrow. Label the statements M for *main idea*, B for *too broad*, and N for *too narrow*.

   _____ a. Martial arts have developed from diverse traditions throughout the world.

   _____ b. Capoeira was banned during slavery and even for some decades after slavery ended.

   _____ c. Although banned for centuries, the martial art capoeira is now practiced widely.

Correct Answers, Part A _____

Correct Answers, Part B _____

Total Correct Answers _____

　　　President Truman's Fair Deal

In 1945 Vice President Harry S. Truman became the 33rd president of the United States. He took office as the result of an unusual circumstance. President Franklin D. Roosevelt had died suddenly, just three months into his fourth term. His death left Truman facing a number of challenges.

As World War II came to a close, the U.S. economy slowly moved from wartime production to consumer production. With the high demands of buyers, the slow shift led to a shortage of goods. As a result, prices rose, and the cost of living increased. President Truman feared that the trend might bring about an economic crisis.

Truman worked to stabilize world relations after the war. He also proposed a series of reforms to steady affairs at home. Widely referred to as the Fair Deal, Truman's reforms drew on Roosevelt's famed New Deal policies. The Fair Deal called for a wide array of government-sponsored social programs. The intent of these programs was twofold. They were meant to improve people's lives and ensure the nation's success in a new era.

During his eight years in office, Truman proposed reforms to protect civil rights, extend public benefits, and raise the minimum wage. Although Congress passed some of these bills, most of the reforms failed to become law during Truman's two terms.

Truman was perhaps most successful in implementing civil rights reforms. Soon after World War II, he formed the President's Committee on Civil Rights to look into racial violence in the nation. The report showed much discrimination against African Americans. It also proposed a list of measures to protect civil rights. When Truman received the report, he took action. He used the power of his office to end segregation in the armed forces and outlaw discrimination in the hiring of federal workers. Despite this success, Congress failed to adopt most of the measures outlined in the report while Truman held office.

Truman's aims to extend public benefits met a similar fate. Reforms to raise the minimum wage, fund low-income housing, and extend social security benefits succeeded. However, Congress failed to pass most of the social programs that Truman proposed. In fact, five decades after Truman's Fair Deal, liberals were still calling for a national health-care plan. Although most of his Fair Deal policies did not become law while he was in office, Truman's proposed programs set the stage for liberal reforms for decades to come.

Reading Time _____

Recalling Facts

1. Harry S. Truman became the 33rd president of the United States when
   - ❑ a. he won the election of 1945.
   - ❑ b. President Roosevelt died suddenly.
   - ❑ c. the prior president was impeached.

2. After World War II, President Truman feared an economic crisis because
   - ❑ a. unemployment levels skyrocketed.
   - ❑ b. the nation lost a great deal of money in the war.
   - ❑ c. a shortage in consumer goods caused prices and the cost of living to rise.

3. The Fair Deal called for
   - ❑ a. government-sponsored social programs.
   - ❑ b. tax breaks for the wealthy.
   - ❑ c. voting rights for women and minorities.

4. The President's Committee on Civil Rights found that
   - ❑ a. all Americans enjoyed the same rights.
   - ❑ b. African Americans faced discrimination.
   - ❑ c. Congress was not taking action to protect civil rights.

5. Most of Truman's social programs
   - ❑ a. were proposed by Congress.
   - ❑ b. were adopted by Congress.
   - ❑ c. failed to pass in Congress.

Understanding Ideas

6. Compared with the success of Truman's effort to raise the minimum wage, his call for a national health-care plan received
   - ❑ a. less support.
   - ❑ b. less discussion.
   - ❑ c. faster approval.

7. From his actions related to civil rights, one can infer that Truman
   - ❑ a. promoted racial discrimination.
   - ❑ b. sought to protect the rights of all Americans.
   - ❑ c. ignored the plight of African Americans.

8. From the passage, one can conclude that the primary reason Truman proposed Fair Deal programs was to
   - ❑ a. gain favor with whites in the South.
   - ❑ b. ensure his reelection.
   - ❑ c. avoid economic crisis in the postwar era.

9. It is likely that Truman named his reforms the Fair Deal to
   - ❑ a. make clear that his reforms would bring about world peace in the postwar era.
   - ❑ b. divorce himself from Roosevelt's policies.
   - ❑ c. create an association in people's minds with Roosevelt's popular New Deal program.

10. One can conclude from the passage that Truman's health-care reforms
    - ❑ a. were supported by conservatives and liberals alike.
    - ❑ b. were opposed by conservatives in Congress.
    - ❑ c. had no popular support.

Not long after World War II ended, whites in the South led attacks on several African American veterans. The police in one state beat and blinded a man. In Georgia a white mob cruelly shot two veterans and their wives.

Fueled by racism and segregation, tensions throughout the nation rose dramatically. President Harry S. Truman had founded the President's Committee on Civil Rights. The group issued a report condemning segregation. It expressly attacked the armed forces. Since the Civil War, African Americans had served in military units separate from whites. They were denied advancement in the ranks as well.

The violent attacks in the South and the civil rights report moved Truman to take action. He promptly drew up an order to end segregation in the armed forces. The aim of this order was to ensure that all members of the armed forces received equal treatment without regard to race or religion. Although it took years to set into action, the order was a huge success. In addition, it influenced views on segregation across the country. Today many salute Truman's order as the beginning of the end of separate-but-equal policies in the United States.

1. **Recognizing Words in Context**

   Find the word *segregation* in the passage. One definition below is closest to the meaning of that word. One definition has the opposite or nearly the opposite meaning. The remaining definition has a completely different meaning. Label the definitions C for *closest*, O for *opposite or nearly opposite*, and D for *different*.

   _____ a. integration

   _____ b. congregation

   _____ c. separation

2. **Distinguishing Fact from Opinion**

   Two of the statements below present *facts*, which can be proved. The other statement is an *opinion*, which expresses someone's thoughts or beliefs. Label the statements F for *fact* and O for *opinion*.

   _____ a. Truman's order was in the nation's best interests.

   _____ b. Truman's order ensured that all members of the armed forces would receive equal treatment.

   _____ c. Racism and segregation fueled tensions in the nation.

3. **Keeping Events in Order**

   Number the statements below 1, 2, and 3 to show the order in which the events took place.

   _____ a. Truman's order to end segregation in the armed forces changes the nation's views on the issue.

   _____ b. Soon after World War II, whites in the South attack African American veterans.

   _____ c. President Truman issues an order to end segregation in the armed forces.

4. **Making Correct Inferences**

   Two of the statements below are correct *inferences,* or reasonable guesses. They are based on information in the passage. The other statement is an incorrect, or faulty, inference. Label the statements C for *correct* inference and F for *faulty* inference.

   _____ a. Truman's order alone ended segregation.

   _____ b. Truman's order had a positive impact on civil rights for African Americans.

   _____ c. The order to end segregation in the armed forces was not Truman's only contribution to civil rights during his presidency.

5. **Understanding Main Ideas**

   One of the statements below expresses the main idea of the passage. One statement is too general, or too broad. The other explains only part of the passage; it is too narrow. Label the statements M for *main idea,* B for *too broad,* and N for *too narrow.*

   _____ a. Truman established the President's Committee on Civil Rights.

   _____ b. When racial tensions fueled by segregation mounted, Truman issued an order to end such practices in the armed forces.

   _____ c. As president, Truman made important contributions in many areas, including civil rights and social welfare.

   Correct Answers, Part A _____

   Correct Answers, Part B _____

   Total Correct Answers _____

From prehistory to the present, humankind has used and developed utensils for eating. People in many cultures use the age-old custom of carrying food to the mouth by hand. Other methods include the use of chopsticks or a knife, spoon, and fork.

Prehistoric peoples were the first to use knives and spoons. They scraped or tore apart meat with pieces of flint, shell, and bone. For spoons they used shells and chips of wood to scoop food to the mouth. With time they began to fashion their own utensils from these materials. They carved flint into sharp blades and made spoons from clay, bone, ivory, and horn. As soon as people learned to work with metals, they began to make metal eating utensils. They cut food with knives. They also used the pointed tip of the blade to spear food and lift it to the mouth. In the Middle Ages in Europe, people carried their own knives for eating. The hosts supplied spoons for their guests. Until very recently, most people in Europe and the United States ate with only knives and spoons.

The ancient Greeks and Romans used large, two-pronged forks when cutting and serving food. However, people of the time did not eat with forks. Perhaps the first people to use forks for eating were the royal families of the Middle East. Like earlier serving forks, these seventh-century forks had just two tines. Although people introduced these forks to European cultures in later centuries, most people in Europe thought forks were unnecessary. After hundreds of years, only the wealthy were using them. With time, however, a four-pronged version of the fork gained widespread favor. Today, people use the fork, knife, and spoon as the basic set of Western eating utensils.

These three implements are common eating utensils in many parts of the world. However, most cultures in East Asia use chopsticks. The use of chopsticks originated in China nearly 5,000 years ago. It came about, perhaps, from the custom of using two twigs to pick up hot food. Because the Chinese chop food into small pieces before cooking it, they do not need knives at the table as Westerners do. The use of two long, narrow sticks held between the fingers of one hand is sufficient for raising bite-size morsels of food to the mouth. The only other eating utensil required is a spoon for soups.

Reading Time _____

Recalling Facts

1. Humankind has used and developed utensils for eating
   - ❏ a. since the Middle Ages.
   - ❏ b. only in recent times.
   - ❏ c. from prehistory to the present.

2. Prehistoric peoples were the first to use
   - ❏ a. knives and spoons.
   - ❏ b. chopsticks.
   - ❏ c. bowls.

3. In ancient times, people used two-pronged forks
   - ❏ a. as gardening tools.
   - ❏ b. to spear food and lift it to the mouth.
   - ❏ c. when cutting and serving food.

4. For hundreds of years after the fork was introduced in Europe, people did not use it because they thought it was
   - ❏ a. dangerous.
   - ❏ b. unnecessary.
   - ❏ c. barbaric.

5. The basic set of East Asian eating utensils today consists of
   - ❏ a. a knife and a spoon.
   - ❏ b. chopsticks and a spoon.
   - ❏ c. a knife, a spoon, and a fork.

Understanding Ideas

6. One can infer from the passage that the oldest method of eating was with
   - ❏ a. a spoon.
   - ❏ b. the hands.
   - ❏ c. chopsticks.

7. From the passage, one can conclude that the first eating utensils were
   - ❏ a. objects readily available.
   - ❏ b. complex inventions.
   - ❏ c. sturdy metal tools.

8. It is likely that people in cultures in which chopsticks are used
   - ❏ a. never use knives.
   - ❏ b. use knives only when eating.
   - ❏ c. use knives only to prepare food.

9. It is likely that some early cultures relied on chopsticks while others relied on knives and spoons because of
   - ❏ a. different ways of preparing food.
   - ❏ b. the lack or presence of metals for tools.
   - ❏ c. different artistic traditions.

10. Compared with East Asian cultures, Western cultures utilize
    - ❏ a. fewer kitchen utensils for cooking.
    - ❏ b. larger spoons.
    - ❏ c. a wider variety of eating utensils.

How to Use Chopsticks

People in many parts of Asia have been eating with chopsticks for thousands of years. The cuisine of these cultures is prepared in bite-size morsels. This is done so that the food can be eaten easily with chopsticks. To learn to eat with chopsticks, one must learn the proper way to hold the utensils and the proper etiquette for their use.

To hold the utensils, cradle the top portion of one chopstick between the thumb and the index finger, letting the lower portion rest on the ring finger just below the fingertip. Next, grasp the second chopstick between the tips of the thumb, index finger, and middle finger. As the first chopstick remains stationary, one manipulates the second chopstick to clutch bits of food. Be sure that the ends of the chopsticks are level.

When using chopsticks, it is important to follow rules of etiquette. When eating Western style, one would not spear a piece of food with a knife and lift it to the mouth. It is just as improper to spear food with chopsticks. It is also considered repugnant to lick the ends of chopsticks. Finally, one should never stand chopsticks in a bowl of rice or pass food with chopsticks, as both acts resemble funeral rituals. By following these rules, one can enjoy a satisfying meal without offending the hosts.

1. **Recognizing Words in Context**

   Find the word *repugnant* in the passage. One definition below is closest to the meaning of that word. One definition has the opposite or nearly the opposite meaning. The remaining definition has a completely different meaning. Label the definitions C for *closest*, O for *opposite or nearly opposite*, and D for *different*.

   _____ a. pleasant

   _____ b. distasteful

   _____ c. stylish

2. **Distinguishing Fact from Opinion**

   Two of the statements below present *facts*, which can be proved. The other statement is an *opinion*, which expresses someone's thoughts or beliefs. Label the statements F for *fact* and O for *opinion*.

   _____ a. People in many parts of Asia have been eating with chopsticks for thousands of years.

   _____ b. Chopsticks are easy to use.

   _____ c. There are rules of etiquette for using chopsticks.

3. Keeping Events in Order

Number the statements below 1, 2, and 3 to show the order in which the events are to take place.

_____ a. Hold the first chopstick stationary while manipulating the second chopstick to clutch bits of food.

_____ b. Grasp the second chopstick between the tips of the thumb, index finger, and middle finger.

_____ c. Cradle one chopstick between the thumb and index finger so that the lower portion rests on the ring finger.

4. Making Correct Inferences

Two of the statements below are correct *inferences,* or reasonable guesses. They are based on information in the passage. The other statement is an incorrect, or faulty, inference. Label the statements C for *correct* inference and F for *faulty* inference.

_____ a. Improper use of chopsticks is considered bad manners.

_____ b. To use chopsticks properly, one simply needs to learn the proper way to hold them.

_____ c. Some rules of etiquette probably apply to the use of Western utensils as well as to the use of chopsticks.

5. Understanding Main Ideas

One of the statements below expresses the main idea of the passage. One statement is too general, or too broad. The other explains only part of the passage; it is too narrow. Label the statements M for *main idea*, B for *too broad*, and N for *too narrow*.

_____ a. Humankind has used and developed eating utensils from prehistory to the present.

_____ b. Etiquette is essential for the proper use of chopsticks.

_____ c. To use chopsticks correctly, one must learn both technique and proper etiquette.

Correct Answers, Part A _____

Correct Answers, Part B _____

Total Correct Answers _____

The Minoans: A Forgotten People

The first advanced culture in ancient Greece was the Minoan culture. For thousands of years, knowledge of these people survived only in Greek myth. In the late nineteenth century, archeologists began to unearth ruins. This inspired Arthur Evans to begin digging on the island of Crete near mainland Greece. On a dig in Knossos, Evans found an ancient labyrinthine palace. Experts think that it was the palace of King Minos, a central figure in many Greek myths.

The palace that Evans unearthed a century ago was the first proof of Minoan culture. With his team, he uncovered a vast structure, varied works of art, and many hieroglyphic records. These finds, together with later finds, comprise all that experts know about Minoan culture.

From the evidence experts gathered, it is clear that the Minoans were ahead of their time. The mazelike palace at Knossos was five floors high with hundreds of rooms. Buildings throughout the ancient city had plumbing and flush toilets. Stone pavement lined the surface of the roads. In addition, the Minoans possessed a highly developed naval fleet for long-distance trade. Although not yet decoded, written script on clay tablets appears to list trade accounts. These records confirm the central role of commerce in the culture.

Expert analysis of the evidence also offers insight into some aspects of Minoan society. Experts believe that a male monarch and mostly female priests ruled the government and controlled trade. Ruins and artwork suggest that people of all classes enjoyed a high degree of social and gender equality. Religious icons show that Minoans worshipped bulls, the natural world, and many female gods.

An unusual feature of Minoan culture was the pursuit of leisure interests. Sports and visual arts were central to Minoan life. Boxing and bull jumping, a sport in which players vaulted over live bulls, were popular. Although bull jumping may have served some ritual purpose, experts believe that it was done mostly for fun. Similarly, although some works of art showed political and religious themes, other works served only as pleasant décor. Some experts think that the wealth derived from trade allowed for such leisure in sports and the arts.

The Minoans met their demise after a series of natural disasters. Experts believe that a group from the Greek mainland capitalized on these events and took over the island.

Reading Time _____

Recalling Facts

1. The Minoan culture was the first advanced culture in
   - ❑ a. ancient Greece.
   - ❑ b. ancient Africa.
   - ❑ c. the ancient Americas.

2. The first proof of Minoan culture unearthed by Arthur Evans a century ago was
   - ❑ a. an ancient palace.
   - ❑ b. a large ship.
   - ❑ c. a clay vase.

3. The central role of trade in Minoan culture is confirmed by
   - ❑ a. the ruins of ancient factories.
   - ❑ b. the size of the king's palace.
   - ❑ c. accounting records and the size of the naval fleet.

4. Leisure interests central to Minoan life were
   - ❑ a. hunting.
   - ❑ b. sports and art.
   - ❑ c. sailing.

5. The Minoan culture met its demise
   - ❑ a. when King Minos died.
   - ❑ b. after a series of natural disasters.
   - ❑ c. as soon as power was seized from the monarchy.

Understanding Ideas

6. The Minoans lived
   - ❑ a. thousands of years ago.
   - ❑ b. a few hundred years ago.
   - ❑ c. about 100 years ago.

7. One can conclude from the five-story palace, indoor plumbing, and paved roads that the Minoans
   - ❑ a. relied heavily on slave labor.
   - ❑ b. had an advanced civilization.
   - ❑ c. had a very small population.

8. One can conclude from the passage that knowledge of the Minoan culture has been gained from each of the following sources except
   - ❑ a. myth.
   - ❑ b. ancient documents explaining their way of life.
   - ❑ c. artifacts.

9. It is likely that warlike people from mainland Greece were able to take over the Minoans because
   - ❑ a. trade had collapsed.
   - ❑ b. the Minoan military was not able to defend the large island.
   - ❑ c. a series of natural disasters weakened the Minoan power to resist invasion.

10. Which of the following statements best describes the main idea?
    - ❑ a. The wealth Minoans gained from trade allowed for the pursuit of leisure interests.
    - ❑ b. Greek myth inspired archeologists to excavate sites thought to be ancient cities.
    - ❑ c. The artifacts and structures unearthed by archeologists in Crete provide insight into the Minoan culture.

12 B Slaying the Minotaur: A Greek Legend

King Minos stood on the shores of Crete, awaiting the ship from Athens that carried seven young men and seven maidens. They were to be food for the Minotaur—a creature, half-man and half-bull, that lived in the labyrinth below the palace.

In Athens parents grieved as their children boarded the ship bearing the black sails of mourning. Seeing their anguish, Theseus, son of the king of Athens, devised a plan to end this tribute of human flesh. He would go in place of one of the young men and slay the Minotaur. If he succeeded, he would return with the ship's white sails raised.

When the ship reached Crete, Minos and his daughter Ariadne escorted the prisoners to their cells. Ariadne had fallen in love with Theseus, and she proposed a plan as they walked. If Theseus would take her away and marry her, she would help him slay the Minotaur.

That night, Ariadne freed Theseus. After Theseus killed the Minotaur, the goddess Athena came to him in a dream and told him to leave Ariadne behind. Because of his grief over having to abandon Ariadne, Theseus forgot to replace the black sails with white ones.

When the king of Athens saw the black-sailed ship returning, he imagined his son dead, and in grief he fell off a cliff into the sea. The loss of their king caused the people of Athens to mourn anew.

1. **Recognizing Words in Context**

   Find the word *anguish* in the passage. One definition below is closest to the meaning of that word. One definition has the opposite or nearly the opposite meaning. The remaining definition has a completely different meaning. Label the definitions C for *closest*, O for *opposite or nearly opposite,* and D for *different.*

   _____ a. anger

   _____ b. suffering

   _____ c. delight

2. **Distinguishing Fact from Opinion**

   Two of the statements below present *facts,* which can be proved. The other statement is an *opinion,* which expresses someone's thoughts or beliefs. Label the statements F for *fact* and O for *opinion.*

   _____ a. Theseus devises a plan to end the suffering of his people.

   _____ b. Ariadne assists Theseus in his mission to slay the Minotaur.

   _____ c. Minos is a cruel king.

3. Keeping Events in Order

Number the statements below 1, 2, and 3 to show the order in which the events took place.

_____ a. Theseus slays the Minotaur and escapes to his ship with the other prisoners.

_____ b. Thinking that his son is dead, the king of Athens falls off a cliff and dies.

_____ c. Theseus forgets to raise the white sails.

4. Making Correct Inferences

Two of the statements below are correct *inferences,* or reasonable guesses. They are based on information in the passage. The other statement is an incorrect, or faulty, inference. Label the statements C for *correct* inference and F for *faulty* inference.

_____ a. Theseus cannot become king because his mistake has caused the death of his father.

_____ b. Theseus's forgeting to raise the white sails causes his father's death.

_____ c. The tribute of human flesh is a tax or payment required by King Minos.

5. Understanding Main Ideas

One of the statements below expresses the main idea of the passage. One statement is too general, or too broad. The other explains only part of the passage; it is too narrow. Label the statements M for *main idea,* B for *too broad,* and N for *too narrow.*

_____ a. Ariadne falls in love with Theseus and agrees to help him slay the Minotaur.

_____ b. Kings, queens, creatures, and gods are the subjects of many ancient Greek writings and myths.

_____ c. Theseus ends the suffering of his people by killing the Minotaur but causes his father's death when he forgets to raise the white sails upon his return.

Correct Answers, Part A _____

Correct Answers, Part B _____

Total Correct Answers _____

Lobbying: What It Is and How It Works

Lobbying occurs when a person or a group tries to influence government decisions. A lobbyist may be an expert paid for an opinion, a group spokesperson, a member of government, or a concerned citizen. Lobbyists work to affect policy at city, state, and federal levels. They express to officials their views on key issues, working to protect or advance their own interests or those of the public. Lobbies provide a crucial link between the public and the government. These groups urge officials to take a stand on issues of concern.

In the United States, lobbying takes many forms. People lobby by writing letters to express their views on key issues. The president lobbies for a policy change by writing members of Congress a memo. Perhaps the most common form of lobbying takes place when paid experts express the views and interests of their groups to members of Congress.

Paid experts may lobby for one group or a number of clients. As paid lobbyists, their job is to reach members of government. They attempt to persuade public officials to take a stand on specific issues. To do so, lobbyists gather and present detailed data about the matter at hand. They construct arguments to support the cause of the interest groups for which they lobby. Then they distribute pamphlets, speak at meetings, and discuss the matter in private with officials.

Interest groups—that is, groups formed to address specific concerns or interests—also employ indirect means to sway officials. Most often interest groups use the media to achieve their goals. Through ads and the press, groups alert the public to their cause. This tactic rallies public support. As a result, citizens express their support of the issue to officials. Public backing strengthens the power that interest groups have to influence officials about government decisions.

Besides public support, interest groups also need to have strong bonds with officials in order to succeed. To build these bonds, interest groups often donate money to campaigns and support the officials who back their cause. Although this system is standard practice, many believe it is in dire need of reform. At its best, lobbying is a vital link between government and the public it serves. At its worst, it promotes the special interests of wealthy groups and big business without regard to the good of the public in general.

Reading Time _____

Recalling Facts

1. Lobbying occurs when a person or a group tries to
   - ❏ a. increase company sales.
   - ❏ b. win an election.
   - ❏ c. influence government decisions.

2. The job of paid lobbyists is to
   - ❏ a. recruit new service members to the armed forces.
   - ❏ b. convince officials to take a stand on certain issues.
   - ❏ c. consider all sides of an issue.

3. Perhaps the most common form of lobbying occurs when
   - ❏ a. paid experts express their interests to Congress members.
   - ❏ b. the president sends memos to Congress.
   - ❏ c. the public writes letters to officials.

4. To succeed, lobbyists need to have
   - ❏ a. strong bonds with officials.
   - ❏ b. the complete support of the public.
   - ❏ c. hundreds of paid experts.

5. In _____, lobbying promotes the special interests of wealthy groups and big business without regard to the public good.
   - ❏ a. all cases
   - ❏ b. its worst form
   - ❏ c. its best form

Understanding Ideas

6. From the passage, one can infer that each of the following is an example of lobbying except
   - ❏ a. paid experts' urging a senator to support a new education bill.
   - ❏ b. a citizen's letter to the mayor about the rising crime rate.
   - ❏ c. employees' request of a raise from their employer.

7. One can conclude from the passage that one powerful way to influence public opinion is by
   - ❏ a. holding rallies.
   - ❏ b. discussing issues with members of government.
   - ❏ c. using various forms of media.

8. In order to succeed, a paid lobbyist likely needs to be
   - ❏ a. an effective speaker.
   - ❏ b. a humorous person.
   - ❏ c. an honest person.

9. From the passage, one can conclude that the public needs
   - ❏ a. to protect the interests of big business.
   - ❏ b. to have effective ways to communicate with government.
   - ❏ c. to ignore special-interest groups.

10. Which of the following best describes the author's view of lobbying?
   - ❏ a. Lobbyists are corrupt.
   - ❏ b. Standard practices of lobbyists favor those who can pay for government support.
   - ❏ c. Protecting the good of the public is the foremost concern of lobbies.

13 B Lobbying Practices and the Need for Reform

Lobbying practices in the United States have long set public interests at odds with special interests. The use of money to win favor in Congress for the interests of big business has been a problem for more than a century. In the late 1800s, such practices influenced lawmakers to pass a number of bills that protected the profits of big business. A few of them also provided roads, schools, and jobs that benefited the public. Most, however, served big business without regard for the public good. As the result of the work of lobby groups, bills were passed that kept utility rates high. In contrast, bills to establish an eight-hour workday were defeated.

During the twentieth century, lawmakers passed some bills that reformed lobbying practices. Current law requires lobbies to register and report all donations. Campaigns also must report any donations received. Despite these attempts at reform, not much has changed. The laws are easy to evade and are rarely enforced.

Perhaps the most effective reform efforts have come from public-interest lobbies. These groups protect the common good by imposing public pressure on lawmakers to oppose bills that profit big business. Other groups, such as Common Cause, tackle the issue head on. They lobby for campaign reform and regulations for lobby groups in an effort to improve the system.

1. **Recognizing Words in Context**

   Find the word *evade* in the passage. One definition below is closest to the meaning of that word. One definition has the opposite or nearly the opposite meaning. The remaining definition has a completely different meaning. Label the definitions C for *closest*, O for *opposite or nearly opposite*, and D for *different*.

   _____ a. avoid

   _____ b. disappear

   _____ c. follow

2. **Distinguishing Fact from Opinion**

   Two of the statements below present *facts*, which can be proved. The other statement is an *opinion*, which expresses someone's thoughts or beliefs. Label the statements F for *fact* and O for *opinion*.

   _____ a. Current law requires lobbies to register and report all donations.

   _____ b. The public would be better off without lobby groups.

   _____ c. Private-business lobby groups often use money to win favor in Congress.

3. Keeping Events in Order

Number the statements below 1, 2, and 3 to show the order in which the events took place.

_____ a. Because lobbying practices changed little, public-interest lobbies put pressure on lawmakers to reform the system.

_____ b. As a result of lobbying, lawmakers passed bills to keep utility rates high and defeated bills to protect workers.

_____ c. Lawmakers tried to curb corruption by requiring lobbies to register and report donations.

4. Making Correct Inferences

Two of the statements below are correct _inferences,_ or reasonable guesses. They are based on information in the passage. The other statement is an incorrect, or faulty, inference. Label the statements C for _correct_ inference and F for _faulty_ inference.

_____ a. Using money to win favor in Congress for big-business interests is still a problem.

_____ b. Some lobbying practices are corrupt.

_____ c. The special interests of private business never benefit the public.

5. Understanding Main Ideas

One of the statements below expresses the main idea of the passage. One statement is too general, or too broad. The other explains only part of the passage; it is too narrow. Label the statements M for _main idea_, B for _too broad_, and N for _too narrow_.

_____ a. Public-interest reform efforts attempt to change corrupt lobbying practices.

_____ b. Lobbying is a long-standing practice that occurs when a person or group attempts to influence government decisions.

_____ c. Lawmakers have passed bills that favor big business.

Correct Answers, Part A _____

Correct Answers, Part B _____

Total Correct Answers _____

The U.S. Congress and Its Role in Government

As outlined in the United States Constitution, there are three branches of government. These three branches are the legislative branch, the executive branch, and the judicial branch.

The legislature, the branch of government that makes laws, is the U.S. Congress. The Senate and the House of Representatives are the two bodies of Congress. Both consist of members elected by the citizens of their states. Members of both the House and the Senate form many committees. The committees address important issues such as finance, energy, and health. The Congress has a number of duties. It collects taxes, raises and allocates funds, regulates commerce, and supports the armed forces.

The main function of Congress, however, is the making of laws. First, a member of Congress proposes a bill outlining the law. The idea for the bill may come from the president, a lobbyist, or members of Congress. Once a lawmaker introduces the bill, the proper committee examines, debates, and amends it. The committee may then decide to report the bill to the full House or the Senate. After further debate, members of each body vote on the bill. If the House of Representatives passes the bill, it moves to the Senate for further discussion. If both bodies of Congress pass the bill, the bill moves to the executive branch to be signed into law or vetoed by the president. A veto from the president can prevent a bill from becoming law, unless Congress can pass the bill a second time with a two-thirds majority in each house. Once a bill is law, however, the Supreme Court has the power to revoke the law if it finds that law unconstitutional. In this way, the executive and judicial branches check the lawmaking power of Congress.

Although the structure and duties of the Senate and the House are alike in many ways, essential differences exist. The Senate is made up of two senators from each state. Each senator serves a term of six years. In the House, representatives serve terms of only two years. The House is much larger than the Senate because the number of representatives per state is determined by the population of the state. House members introduce all revenue bills and initiate impeachment proceedings. In contrast, the Senate holds impeachment hearings, ratifies treaties, and appoints certain officials—such as Supreme Court justices. With its many duties, the U.S. Congress plays a vital role in the government.

Reading Time _____

Recalling Facts

1. In the United States, the three branches of government were created by
   - ❑ a. popular vote.
   - ❑ b. the U.S. Constitution.
   - ❑ c. Congress.

2. The two bodies of Congress are the Senate and
   - ❑ a. the Supreme Court.
   - ❑ b. the House of Representatives.
   - ❑ c. the executive branch.

3. The main function of Congress is
   - ❑ a. making laws.
   - ❑ b. appointing Supreme Court justices.
   - ❑ c. collecting taxes.

4. Each body of Congress consists of
   - ❑ a. a chair, a secretary, and a treasurer.
   - ❑ b. a president, a judge, and representatives.
   - ❑ c. representatives elected by citizens in their states.

5. If both bodies of Congress pass a bill, the bill moves to the executive branch to be signed or vetoed by
   - ❑ a. the Senate.
   - ❑ b. the Supreme Court.
   - ❑ c. the president.

Understanding Ideas

6. One can conclude from the passage that both bodies of Congress have the same
   - ❑ a. length of term for members.
   - ❑ b. way of electing members.
   - ❑ c. number of members.

7. From the passage, one can conclude that for a bill to become law it must
   - ❑ a. pass in both the House and the Senate.
   - ❑ b. be signed by a Supreme Court justice.
   - ❑ c. be approved by the nation's citizens.

8. If a bill introduced in the House never reached the Senate, it is likely that
   - ❑ a. the House voted against the bill.
   - ❑ b. the president vetoed the bill.
   - ❑ c. the Supreme Court found the bill unconstitutional.

9. A member of Congress who is one of two representatives from her state and is serving the sixth year of her term is
   - ❑ a. a member of the House of Representatives.
   - ❑ b. a senator.
   - ❑ c. a Supreme Court justice.

10. It is likely that the president's power to veto a bill and the Supreme Court's power to revoke an unconstitutional law serve to
    - ❑ a. delay unnecessary legislation.
    - ❑ b. strengthen the link between the public and government.
    - ❑ c. check Congress's lawmaking powers.

14   B   How to Write a Letter to a Member of Congress

Letters are the chief form of contact between members of Congress and their constituents. To write an effective letter to one's representatives, it is important to follow both format and content guidelines.

A letter to a member of Congress should follow a business format. First, address the letter to the official, using the title *The Honorable* before the person's name. Then begin the letter with *Dear Senator* for a member of the Senate or *Dear Representative* for a member of the House. Be sure to include a return address to which the official can reply.

The key aspect of the letter is the content. State the purpose of the letter and define the issue of concern in the first paragraph. Then, in the body of the letter, be sure to discuss the issue and defend one viewpoint. It may also be appropriate to address how the issue affects the Congress member's home state. Finally, request that the member of Congress take specific action with regard to the issue.

Although this seems like a great deal to address, it is crucial to keep the letter succinct. Members of Congress prefer one-page letters that focus clearly on one issue. They are more likely to read and respond to letters that follow these guidelines.

1. Recognizing Words in Context

Find the word *succinct* in the passage. One definition below is closest to the meaning of that word. One definition has the opposite or nearly the opposite meaning. The remaining definition has a completely different meaning. Label the definitions C for *closest*, O for *opposite or nearly opposite*, and D for *different*.

_____ a. concise

_____ b. rambling

_____ c. courteous

2. Distinguishing Fact from Opinion

Two of the statements below present *facts*, which can be proved. The other statement is an *opinion*, which expresses someone's thoughts or beliefs. Label the statements F for *fact* and O for *opinion*.

_____ a. Contacting members of Congress is a waste of time.

_____ b. Letters are the primary form of contact between members of Congress and their constituents.

_____ c. The title *The Honorable* is used for a congressperson.

3. Keeping Events in Order

Number the statements below 1, 2, and 3 to show the order in which the events take place.

_____ a. Address the letter using the title *The Honorable* before the official's name.

_____ b. State the purpose of the letter in the first paragraph.

_____ c. Request that the member of Congress take specific action with regard to the issue of concern.

4. Making Correct Inferences

Two of the statements below are correct *inferences*, or reasonable guesses. They are based on information in the passage. The other statement is an incorrect, or faulty, inference. Label the statements C for *correct* inference and F for *faulty* inference.

_____ a. Members of Congress receive a great deal of mail from their constituents.

_____ b. It is unlikely that a member of Congress will reply to a constituent's letter.

_____ c. Letter writers often seek to influence their representatives on important issues.

5. Understanding Main Ideas

One of the statements below expresses the main idea of the passage. One statement is too general, or too broad. The other explains only part of the passage; it is too narrow. Label the statements M for *main idea*, B for *too broad*, and N for *too narrow*.

_____ a. It is important to keep letters to representatives succinct.

_____ b. An effective letter to a member of Congress complies with both format and content guidelines.

_____ c. Citizens should communicate with members of Congress.

Correct Answers, Part A _____

Correct Answers, Part B _____

Total Correct Answers _____

Louisa May Alcott: Author and Civil War Nurse

Little Women is the best-known work of author Louisa May Alcott. Published after the end of the Civil War, the book is based on the lives of the author and her sisters. Although it was by far her most successful work, it was not her first.

Alcott's writing career began at the age of 20 with the publication of her poem "Sunlight." Throughout her early career, she wrote many poems and short stories for magazines. At the age of 22, she began to write fairy tales, romantic thrillers, and other novels, mostly to earn money. At a time when few opportunities were open to women, Alcott supported women's right to work. With her meager income, she had long provided for her family.

Upon the outbreak of the Civil War, Alcott seized the chance to defend a cause in which she deeply believed—the abolition of slavery. At the age of 30, she joined the war effort. She had originally wished to serve as a soldier. However, women were not allowed in battle at that time. As a result, armed with skills gained in nursing her family, she became a Civil War nurse. Alcott's work as a nurse served as a milestone in her career.

In December of 1862, she left New England to work in the Union Hotel Hospital in Washington, D.C. On her first day, she watched a man die and nursed a soldier who had a lung wound. After the Battle of Fredericksburg, hundreds of wounded soldiers flooded the converted hotel. There were few supplies, and doctors performed surgery without painkillers. The hospital lacked a sanitary system, and the conditions for patients and staff were dreadful. Within a few weeks, Alcott herself became so ill with typhoid pneumonia that she nearly died. She returned home and recovered slowly over a period of months.

As soon as her health improved, Alcott started a new project. The letters she had sent home became the basis of a newspaper series about her experience as a Civil War nurse. She wrote poignantly about her tasks, the wounded soldiers she tended, and the awful conditions they faced. The series was a success, and publishers began to seek her out. They published the series as the book *Hospital Sketches,* which received praise from readers and critics alike. Although her best-known work was yet to come, the success of *Hospital Sketches* marked the achievement of her dream to become a popular author.

Reading Time _____

Recalling Facts

1. Louisa May Alcott was
   - ❏ a. a teacher.
   - ❏ b. a soldier.
   - ❏ c. an author.

2. Early in her career, Alcott wrote
   - ❏ a. poems and short stories for magazines.
   - ❏ b. her best-known work, *Little Women*.
   - ❏ c. a book about her experiences as a nurse.

3. During the Civil War, Alcott joined the war effort as a
   - ❏ a. journalist.
   - ❏ b. soldier.
   - ❏ c. nurse.

4. Conditions for patients and staff at the Union Hotel Hospital during the Civil War were
   - ❏ a. dreadful.
   - ❏ b. sanitary.
   - ❏ c. peaceful.

5. With the publication of *Hospital Sketches,* Alcott achieved
   - ❏ a. her goal to abolish slavery.
   - ❏ b. popular fame as an author.
   - ❏ c. her first income from writing.

Understanding Ideas

6. During the Civil War, it is likely that Alcott fell ill with typhoid pneumonia as a result of
   - ❏ a. a family history of the disease.
   - ❏ b. unsanitary hospital conditions.
   - ❏ c. malnourishment.

7. Her dedication as a nurse reveals that Alcott was probably
   - ❏ a. a hardworking, caring person.
   - ❏ b. an independent, yet selfish, person.
   - ❏ c. a reckless, daring person.

8. Compared with her early romantic thrillers and sensational novels, *Hospital Sketches* was
   - ❏ a. a less successful work.
   - ❏ b. a more serious work.
   - ❏ c. a more imaginative work.

9. One can conclude from the passage that, as a Civil War nurse, Alcott supported such causes as
   - ❏ a. conservation and protection of wilderness areas.
   - ❏ b. copyright laws to protect authors.
   - ❏ c. the abolition of slavery and the right of women to work.

10. It is likely that Alcott's success grew with such works as *Hospital Sketches* and *Little Women* because her writing
    - ❏ a. gained sensitivity as she recounted her own experiences.
    - ❏ b. grew more concise as she matured.
    - ❏ c. became a career rather than a hobby.

15   B   Civil War Nurses: Pioneers in Their Field

When the Civil War broke out in 1861, there were few trained nurses in the nation. At the time, only doctors provided medical care to the ill or injured. However, the war brought large numbers of casualties, and doctors came to rely more and more on the aid of war nurses. Although some religious orders had been training women as nurses for years, most nurses in the war had no training at all. During the war, women from both sides used basic skills and common sense in providing comfort and care to the wounded.

Civil War nurses performed a number of tasks in their service. They often risked their lives for the war effort. Nurses worked in unclean hospitals, aided the wounded on the battlefield, and transported supplies to the front line. They also took charge of the medical-relief effort as a whole. Nurses founded hospitals, trained and supervised volunteers, and gathered funds and supplies.

After the war, many Civil War nurses persisted in their work. Not only did Civil War nurses serve the war effort; they acted as pioneers in the emerging field of nursing. Nursing handbooks, training schools, relief organizations, and more hospitals were just a few of their postwar achievements.

1. **Recognizing Words in Context**

   Find the word *persisted* in the passage. One definition below is closest to the meaning of that word. One definition has the opposite or nearly the opposite meaning. The remaining definition has a completely different meaning. Label the definitions C for *closest,* O for *opposite or nearly opposite,* and D for *different.*

   _____ a. inspired

   _____ b. continued

   _____ c. ceased

2. **Distinguishing Fact from Opinion**

   Two of the statements below present *facts,* which can be proved. The other statement is an *opinion,* which expresses someone's thoughts or beliefs. Label the statements F for *fact* and O for *opinion.*

   _____ a. Few Civil War nurses had prior training.

   _____ b. Civil War nurses risked their lives for the war effort.

   _____ c. Civil War nurses had their greatest impact after the war, as they developed the nursing profession.

3. Keeping Events in Order

Number the statements below 1, 2, and 3 to show the order in which the events took place.

_____ a. Nursing handbooks, training schools, and hospitals were some accomplishments of Civil War nurses.

_____ b. During the Civil War, most nurses used basic skills and common sense in providing care.

_____ c. Religious orders began training women as nurses.

4. Making Correct Inferences

Two of the statements below are correct *inferences,* or reasonable guesses. They are based on information in the passage. The other statement is an incorrect, or faulty, inference. Label the statements C for *correct* inference and F for *faulty* inference.

_____ a. Women could do little to aid the war effort without a proper nursing education.

_____ b. Because many men were occupied with fighting the war, Civil War nurses took on responsibilities previously entrusted to men.

_____ c. The work performed by Civil War nurses helped to bring professionalism to the field of nursing.

5. Understanding Main Ideas

One of the statements below expresses the main idea of the passage. One statement is too general, or too broad. The other explains only part of the passage; it is too narrow. Label the statements M for *main idea,* B for *too broad,* and N for *too narrow.*

_____ a. Throughout time, women have taken on various roles to aid war efforts.

_____ b. Women on both sides of the war risked their lives to nurse the wounded.

_____ c. The variety of medical relief tasks women performed in the Civil War advanced the newly formed field of nursing.

Correct Answers, Part A _____

Correct Answers, Part B _____

Total Correct Answers _____

Coal Mining, Past and Present

The most abundant of the fossil fuels is coal, which forms over millions of years from the remains of plants. People have been using coal for heat energy since ancient times. With basic tools, they chipped chunks of coal from exposed seams on the earth's surface. Once they had exhausted these seams, people began to develop new mining techniques to access deeper deposits.

In the late eighteenth century, the Industrial Revolution increased the demand for coal and the need for mines. Soon there were coal mines in almost every region of the United States. The industry created hundreds of thousands of jobs. It played an important role in the nation's early economy. The top coal producer of this era was the state of Pennsylvania.

In these early days, miners cut, drilled, blasted, loaded, and hauled coal without the aid of machinery. The only tools they had were the ones they carried with them. Miners took timber into the tunnel to support the roof in their work area. Then they used picks, drills, and blasting powder to loosen the coal from the rock. To remove coal from the tunnels, they shoveled it into railcars or carts pulled by mules. Although steam power and electric power became available, most manual mining methods persisted well into the twentieth century.

Conditions for coal miners in the early days were treacherous. They worked long hours in cold, damp tunnels with little light. Ventilation was poor, and the miners were at constant risk. Blasting released noxious gases that could make a miner ill or cause an explosion. Blasting also could make the walls and roof of the tunnel unstable. Rock falls claimed many lives. Each year in the coal mines, more than a thousand people died, and tens of thousands were injured.

Over the past 50 years, advances in technology have improved coal-mining techniques. The industry now uses machines for mining tasks. Hydraulic machines support the tunnel roof, sensors control ventilation, and miners can operate equipment by remote control from an office. The new technology offers high yield and superior safety. Fewer than 50 coal miners die per year from work-related accidents. At the same time, these advances have reduced the workforce to one-tenth of its former size. Coal mining still aids the nation's economy and serves its energy needs. Coal is used in the United States today primarily to generate electricity.

Reading Time _____

Recalling Facts

1. A fossil fuel that forms over millions of years from the remains of plants is
   - ❑ a. coal.
   - ❑ b. rock.
   - ❑ c. blasting powder.

2. In the early mining days of the Industrial Revolution, coal miners cut, drilled, blasted, loaded, and hauled coal
   - ❑ a. by remote control from an office.
   - ❑ b. without the aid of machines.
   - ❑ c. from exposed seams on the earth's surface.

3. To loosen coal from the rock, early miners used
   - ❑ a. mules and chains.
   - ❑ b. jackhammers.
   - ❑ c. picks, drills, and blasting powder.

4. Conditions for coal miners in the early days were
   - ❑ a. satisfactory.
   - ❑ b. good.
   - ❑ c. dangerous.

5. Coal-mining techniques have improved over the last 50 years as a result of
   - ❑ a. advances in technology.
   - ❑ b. higher safety standards.
   - ❑ c. dynamite.

Understanding Ideas

6. In addition to creating jobs, it is likely that the early coal-mining industry helped the economy by
   - ❑ a. using manual mining methods.
   - ❑ b. providing fuel for the Industrial Revolution.
   - ❑ c. generating electricity.

7. Compared with manual mining methods, current techniques provide
   - ❑ a. fewer jobs and less coal.
   - ❑ b. more jobs and greater profits.
   - ❑ c. higher yields and greater safety.

8. It is likely that mining-equipment companies invented hydraulic roof supports and sensors to control ventilation in order to
   - ❑ a. improve miners' safety.
   - ❑ b. increase productivity.
   - ❑ c. reduce the labor force.

9. From the passage, one can conclude that a drawback to the advances in the coal-mining industry was
   - ❑ a. the reduction of the workforce.
   - ❑ b. the cost of equipment.
   - ❑ c. lower yields.

10. One can infer from the passage that the coal-mining industry of the future will
    - ❑ a. rebuild its workforce.
    - ❑ b. decrease production.
    - ❑ c. improve safety standards.

Coal-Mining Equipment at Work

The coal-mining industry depends on specialized equipment to attain high yields and ensure worker safety. For both surface and underground mining, the coal industry uses a number of large machines. These machines help miners to prepare the job site, cut the coal from the surrounding rock, and haul the coal away.

In surface mines, workers use large-capacity bulldozers and scrapers to clear the land. Then, after drilling and blasting, they remove debris from the site and begin to cut the coal from its seam. To clear the rubble, miners operate a variety of shovels and dragline machines. Another machine, called the bucket-wheel excavator, loads both debris and coal onto large high-speed conveyor belts.

In underground coal mines, it is necessary to secure the roof of the mine. A piece of equipment called a roof bolter inserts rows of bolts into the rock ceiling. The bolts act like the stones of an arch, helping to buttress the roof. Another device, a radio-controlled mobile roof support, serves as a steel canopy over the work site. All the while, a plowlike shearer mines the coal from the exposed seams. From there a conveyor belt carries the coal to the surface. At each stage, miners are there to operate the equipment and oversee the task.

1. Recognizing Words in Context

Find the word *buttress* in the passage. One definition below is closest to the meaning of that word. One definition has the opposite or nearly the opposite meaning. The remaining definition has a completely different meaning. Label the definitions C for *closest*, O for *opposite or nearly opposite*, and D for *different*.

_____ a. support

_____ b. oppose

_____ c. weaken

2. Distinguishing Fact from Opinion

Two of the statements below present *facts*, which can be proved. The other statement is an *opinion*, which expresses someone's thoughts or beliefs. Label the statements F for *fact* and O for *opinion*.

_____ a. Roof bolters and mobile roof supports secure the mine ceiling.

_____ b. Today modern equipment makes miners' jobs easy and enjoyable.

_____ c. Miners operate equipment and oversee each stage of the mining process.

3. Keeping Events in Order

Number the statements below 1, 2, and 3 to show the order in which the events take place.

_____ a. Bulldozers and scrapers clear the land for a surface mine.

_____ b. A high-speed conveyor belt carries the coal from the mine site.

_____ c. After blasting and drilling, workers operate shovels and draglines to clear and load rubble and coal.

4. Making Correct Inferences

Two of the statements below are correct *inferences,* or reasonable guesses. They are based on information in the passage. The other statement is an incorrect, or faulty, inference. Label the statements C for *correct* inference and F for *faulty* inference.

_____ a. Roof bolters and mobile roof supports protect workers from rock falls.

_____ b. The new equipment prevents all mining accidents.

_____ c. The continuous motion of the plowlike shearer produces a high coal yield.

5. Understanding Main Ideas

One of the statements below expresses the main idea of the passage. One statement is too general, or too broad. The other explains only part of the passage; it is too narrow. Label the statements M for *main idea,* B for *too broad,* and N for *too narrow.*

_____ a. At each stage of the mining process, coal miners operate equipment and oversee the task.

_____ b. Technology has revolutionized the mining industry.

_____ c. The coal-mining industry uses large machines to prepare the job site, cut the coal from the surrounding rock, and haul the coal away.

Correct Answers, Part A _____

Correct Answers, Part B _____

Total Correct Answers _____

The Age of Exploration in Europe took place during the fifteenth and sixteenth centuries. For hundreds of years, European countries had been trading with India, China, and Persia (known today as Iran). During that time, overland routes had become more and more costly. Lured by the prospect of increased trade and profit, royal families throughout Europe hired crews to explore new sea routes that might reach the Indies. Prince Henry the Navigator, of Portugal prompted the first voyages in search of an eastern route. Decades later Spain hired Christopher Columbus to pursue a western route. Similarly, the English sent John Cabot in search of a faster route. No route reached the Indies. However, each new route led to previously unknown lands.

The era's earliest sea explorations, prompted by Henry, progressed slowly. Inspired by advances in navigation and ship design, Henry was keen to explore a realm beyond his known world. The quest began with short journeys into the Atlantic Ocean along the unknown African coast. With each voyage, the crews made new maps. They also gained important maritime knowledge that would inspire future trips. They set up ports of trade in the coastal towns they came across. They found that they could reap profits without reaching the Indies.

Henry hoped to attain another goal. Christians of Portugal and Spain had been embroiled in a long and bitter battle to conquer neighboring Muslims. Henry hoped that the latest sea routes might offer a new point of attack against Islam. He wanted to ensure the triumph of Christianity. Because of the longstanding religious conflict, the Church supported this cause. Church decrees justified the conquest of other lands in order to convert "heathens" to the Christian faith. Later the Spanish sent missionaries to the New World to perform mass conversions.

Each voyage in search of a new route to the Indies resulted in the discovery of once-unknown lands. As the Portuguese had found in Africa, exploration of these lands was far more lucrative than trade in the Indies. Spain and Portugal, the pioneers of the era, quickly gained wealth and power and established large empires. The more lands they conquered and claimed, the more security and power they had in the world. Inspired, and perhaps frightened, by this wealth and power, other nations in Europe set out to stake their claim in the New World. Such exploration continued for centuries to come.

Reading Time _____

Recalling Facts

1. When overland trade routes to the Indies became too costly, Europeans
   - ❏ a. developed the railroad.
   - ❏ b. traded only locally.
   - ❏ c. set out to find sea routes to the Indies.

2. Although the expeditions of Prince Henry the Navigator, Christopher Columbus, and John Cabot did not reach the Indies, each team
   - ❏ a. came upon new lands.
   - ❏ b. circled the globe.
   - ❏ c. became wealthy.

3. The first sea explorations of the era were
   - ❏ a. trips around the world.
   - ❏ b. short journeys along the African coast.
   - ❏ c. long voyages to the Indies.

4. The Church supported Prince Henry's goals because it wanted to
   - ❏ a. reap profits in Africa.
   - ❏ b. ensure the triumph of Christianity.
   - ❏ c. gather maritime knowledge.

5. The wealth and power of Spain and Portugal inspired other nations in Europe to
   - ❏ a. fall into poverty.
   - ❏ b. build up their military.
   - ❏ c. set out to stake their claims in the New World.

Understanding Ideas

6. One can conclude from the passage that the primary reason for fifteenth century exploration was to
   - ❏ a. reach the Indies by sea.
   - ❏ b. gain converts to Christianity.
   - ❏ c. discover new lands.

7. Compared with the ships available to Henry, earlier ship design in Europe was
   - ❏ a. too expensive to be practical.
   - ❏ b. inadequate for long ocean voyages.
   - ❏ c. not encouraged by royal families.

8. One can conclude that
   - ❏ a. royal families were not interested in commercial activities.
   - ❏ b. Europeans were content to conduct trade according to established patterns.
   - ❏ c. the Church's influence was a powerful force in Europe in the fifteenth century.

9. One can conclude from the passage that the early explorers of the fifteenth and sixteenth centuries sought
   - ❏ a. freedom and equality.
   - ❏ b. profit, knowledge, and the triumph of their religion.
   - ❏ c. military allies and peace.

10. Compared with the early voyages of the era, later journeys of exploration were more focused on
    - ❏ a. gaining seafaring knowledge.
    - ❏ b. trade with the new lands encountered.
    - ❏ c. claiming territory and expanding its empire.

17 B   Jacques Cartier's Feats and Failures

In 1534 Jacques Cartier became the first French explorer to lead a voyage to the New World. Cartier was a skilled navigator. His knowledge of the sea led the king of France to believe that Cartier might be able to find a sea route to the Indies.

On this first trip, Cartier sailed northwest into the Atlantic toward Newfoundland. He hoped to find a waterway joining the Atlantic and Pacific Oceans because he believed that future expeditions might use it to reach the Indies. After finding a few small rivers, he came across a large bay near modern-day Quebec, Canada. He believed that it might lead to the Pacific Ocean. He encountered a group of Native people—the Hurons— who told him a fantastical tale. Near their village was a river without end and a land full of riches. He promptly returned to France to prepare a larger expedition.

One year later, Cartier set sail for Canada again. Although he was not able to find the mythical river or the land of riches, he did claim the whole of Canada for the French crown. Cartier had made his way farther into North America than any other European. Although a French colony did not succeed in the harsh land for decades to come, Cartier's journey marked France's possession of the vast territory.

1. **Recognizing Words in Context**

   Find the word *fantastical* in the passage. One definition below is closest to the meaning of that word. One definition has the opposite or nearly the opposite meaning. The remaining definition has a completely different meaning. Label the definitions C for *closest*, O for *opposite or nearly opposite*, and D for *different*.

   _____ a. factual

   _____ b. dreadful

   _____ c. imaginary

2. **Distinguishing Fact from Opinion**

   Two of the statements below present *facts*, which can be proved. The other statement is an *opinion*, which expresses someone's thoughts or beliefs. Label the statements F for *fact* and O for *opinion*.

   _____ a. Claiming Canada was Cartier's most important achievement.

   _____ b. Cartier was the first French explorer to lead a voyage to the New World.

   _____ c. Cartier's journey marked France's possession of Canada.

3. Keeping Events in Order

Number the statements below 1, 2, and 3 to show the order in which the events took place.

_____ a. Cartier explored farther into North America than any European before him.

_____ b. The king of France commissioned Cartier to seek a northwest sea route to the Indies.

_____ c. Cartier found a large bay that he thought might lead to the Pacific Ocean.

4. Making Correct Inferences

Two of the statements below are correct *inferences,* or reasonable guesses. They are based on information in the passage. The other statement is an incorrect, or faulty, inference. Label the statements C for *correct* inference and F for *faulty* inference.

_____ a. In spite of his immediate failures, Cartier's expeditions proved very successful in the long run.

_____ b. Cartier was not able to find the river without end nor the land of riches because neither existed.

_____ c. Cartier's voyages served to found a successful colony in Canada.

5. Understanding Main Ideas

One of the statements below expresses the main idea of the passage. One statement is too general, or too broad. The other explains only part of the passage; it is too narrow. Label the statements M for *main idea,* B for *too broad,* and N for *too narrow.*

_____ a. France did not establish a successful colony in Canada until many decades after Cartier's trips.

_____ b. Although Cartier failed to attain his immediate goals, in the end his expeditions were a huge success.

_____ c. Throughout the fifteenth and sixteenth centuries, European explorers searched for sea routes to the Indies.

Correct Answers, Part A _____

Correct Answers, Part B _____

Total Correct Answers _____

The term *folk art* describes a broad range of creations—from native baskets to sculptures made of recycled cans. For this reason, folk art can be difficult to define. People often confuse folk art with other forms of art, such as outsider art and visionary art. It is true that there is much crossover between these art forms. However, each art form has specific attributes that set it apart from others.

In basic terms, folk art is the art of the people rather than the elite. It exists outside mainstream fine art. Unlike fine art, folk art is not academic in nature. In most cases, the artists who create folk works have not received formal training in art schools. Folk artists may be self-taught, or they may learn from family members, people in their communities, and craft masters. Some folk artists are highly trained artisans or professionals in their field.

The role of tradition and community are the most important defining features of folk art. Tradition may direct the design, the content, or the materials used for a certain work. In many cases, the art form passes from one generation to the next. It may be confined to a specific region or group of people.

Quilting is a folk art that clearly illustrates this link with tradition and community. Standard patterns and materials passed from one generation to the next still inspire quilt making. In addition, quilting is particular to a certain locale—the United States.

Although its definition may seem clear, there is little consensus about what folk art is. Modern folk artists blur the boundaries between tradition and innovation, using old elements in new ways. In today's global society, folk artists are drawing more and more on traditions from a number of regions. Society has also embraced a number of art forms once found only on the fringe.

Outsider art is made up of works by untrained artists who have no concept of art apart from their own creations. Visionary art is an art form in which the artist's inner, rather than aesthetic, voice governs the creation. Within each of these art forms, there is a great deal of overlap. As a result, even experts have a hard time classifying works of art that are outside the mainstream. What was once viewed as folk art just because it was not fine art could now be considered one of any number of art forms.

Reading Time _____

Recalling Facts

1. In basic terms, folk art is
   - ❑ a. the art of children.
   - ❑ b. the art of the people.
   - ❑ c. the art of the elite.

2. Unlike fine art, folk art is not
   - ❑ a. traditional.
   - ❑ b. creative.
   - ❑ c. academic.

3. The most important defining features of folk art are
   - ❑ a. tradition and community.
   - ❑ b. aesthetic voice and skill.
   - ❑ c. color and pattern.

4. Classifying works of art that are outside the mainstream is
   - ❑ a. no easy task.
   - ❑ b. easy for experts.
   - ❑ c. not possible.

5. Art works by untrained artists who have no concept of art apart from their own creations are termed
   - ❑ a. fine art.
   - ❑ b. folk art.
   - ❑ c. outsider art.

Understanding Ideas

6. A work likely to be classified as folk art is
   - ❑ a. a comic strip.
   - ❑ b. a wood carving of a local animal.
   - ❑ c. an ancient Greek sculpture.

7. A weaver who is a folk artist most likely learned the trade by
   - ❑ a. watching "how-to" videos.
   - ❑ b. studying at an academy.
   - ❑ c. working with a master in the community.

8. Compared with an outsider artist, a folk artist is
   - ❑ a. more commonplace.
   - ❑ b. less skilled.
   - ❑ c. less traditional.

9. One can conclude from the passage that the terms *folk art, outsider art,* and *visionary art*
   - ❑ a. describe a single style of art.
   - ❑ b. possess distinct features.
   - ❑ c. share nothing in common.

10. From the passage, one can conclude that with the progress of time folk art has
    - ❑ a. remained unchanged.
    - ❑ b. virtually disappeared.
    - ❑ c. evolved with society.

Quilting: Continuity and Change

In recent decades, a study of folk art in the Blue Ridge Mountains revealed that few women still practiced quilting in the traditional manner. Gone are the days when women used grain sacks, old clothing, and scraps of cloth to make patterns passed from one generation to the next. Women now learn the craft from books, magazines, and classes. They use fabric bought in stores, and they craft new patterns from the old. Have these changes compromised the quilting tradition, or have quilters merely adapted the art form to reflect their own ways of life?

Early on, quilting spread from Euro-American communities to those of African Americans and Native Americans. Each group imbued the art with its own textile traditions. Irregular patterns were common in the quilts of African Americans. Native American quilts featured ribbon work, weaving, and age-old cultural symbols. Current designs reflect these traditions more than ever.

Certainly quilting in the United States has changed. With the use of computerized machines, few quilters hand stitch their works anymore. The pace of life prevents many quilters from working daily on their quilts. Despite the changes in process and design, aspects of the quilting tradition remain. Quilts continue to connect their makers to their families, their communities and cultures, and a rich shared past.

1. **Recognizing Words in Context**

   Find the word *compromised* in the passage. One definition below is closest to the meaning of that word. One definition has the opposite or nearly the opposite meaning. The remaining definition has a completely different meaning. Label the definitions C for *closest*, O for *opposite or nearly opposite*, and D for *different*.

   _____ a. endangered

   _____ b. preserved

   _____ c. improved

2. **Distinguishing Fact from Opinion**

   Two of the statements below present *facts*, which can be proved. The other statement is an *opinion*, which expresses someone's thoughts or beliefs. Label the statements F for *fact* and O for *opinion*.

   _____ a. Most quilters no longer use grain sacks, old clothing, and scraps of cloth to make quilts.

   _____ b. Traditional quilts were superior to modern quilts.

   _____ c. African Americans used their own textile traditions in their quilts.

3. Keeping Events in Order

Two of the statements below describe events that happened at the same time. The other statement describes an event that happened before or after those events. Label them *S* for same time, *B* for before, and *A* for after.

_____ a. Some quilters use computerized machines to stitch their quilts.

_____ b. Quilters learn the craft from books, magazines, and classes.

_____ c. Quilters hand stitch old scraps of cloth into patterns passed from one generation to the next.

4. Making Correct Inferences

Two of the statements below are correct *inferences,* or reasonable guesses. They are based on information in the passage. The other statement is an incorrect, or faulty, inference. Label the statements C for *correct* inference and F for *faulty* inference.

_____ a. The American quilting tradition has died out.

_____ b. The tradition of quilting in the United States continues but has modern features.

_____ c. The significance of quilting has changed little through time.

5. Understanding Main Ideas

One of the statements below expresses the main idea of the passage. One statement is too general, or too broad. The other explains only part of the passage; it is too narrow. Label the statements M for *main idea,* B for *too broad,* and N for *too narrow.*

_____ a. Although the art of quilting has changed a great deal, certain traditional aspects continue.

_____ b. African Americans and Native Americans incorporate their own textile traditions into their quilts.

_____ c. Quilting clearly illustrates the role of tradition and community in folk art.

Correct Answers, Part A _____

Correct Answers, Part B _____

Total Correct Answers _____

Australia's Cultural Development

Australia is the largest island and the smallest continent in the world. It is also a "salad bowl" of ethnic groups and cultures. People from all over the world have come to the South Pacific to become part of its unique society.

Long before Australia became a magnet for immigrants, it was home to its own aborigines. Some experts believe that these ancient people were immigrants themselves. They may have come across land bridges from Asia about 60,000 years ago. The aborigines were hunters and gatherers. They developed a culture in which people respected one other and their environment. The coming of the Europeans soon shattered this peaceful lifestyle.

As early as the 1600s, Dutch and Spanish sailors reported sighting Australia. In 1770 Captain James Cook of Great Britain landed there while searching for Antarctica. He claimed the land, which he named New South Wales, for Great Britain. Upon his return home, he reported that the land would be ideal for settlement.

At first the British government ignored Cook's suggestion. After losing its colonies in North America in the Revolutionary War, however, Great Britain saw a use for Australia. Before the war, the British had exiled many convicts to America. They now needed a new penal colony. John Banks had sailed to Australia with Cook. He thought that Australia might be an ideal choice. It was sparsely settled. It was also a great distance from Great Britain.

The 759 convicts who began the first British settlement on Australia left Great Britain in May 1787 on a fleet of ships called the First Fleet. These convicts faced many hardships. Still, they helped establish a society of free citizens and greatly changed the way the Native people lived. Although the aborigines in due course suffered through disease and the loss of their land, parts of their culture merged with Europe's traditions to create a blend that is unique to Australia.

Over time the British settlement grew. After gold was discovered in 1851, people from all over the world rushed to the continent.

This influx of immigrants continued for years. After World War II, people from Italy, Germany, and Holland came in search of a new life after losing their own homes. In fact, about half a million refugees have fled to Australia since 1945. All of Australia's immigrants brought their customs with them. These practices merged with those of the other residents. Today, Australians pride themselves on their cultural diversity.

Reading Time _____

Recalling Facts

1. The aborigines may have come to Australia about
   - ❑ a. 50,000 years ago.
   - ❑ b. 60,000 years ago.
   - ❑ c. 40,000 years ago.

2. Captain James Cook landed at Australia instead of his original destination, which was
   - ❑ a. New Zealand.
   - ❑ b. the American colonies.
   - ❑ c. Antarctica.

3. Immigration increased greatly when
   - ❑ a. more convicts arrived.
   - ❑ b. gold was discovered.
   - ❑ c. Great Britain lost the American colonies.

4. Australia was thought to be a good location for a penal colony because it was
   - ❑ a. in a tropical latitude.
   - ❑ b. close to the American colonies.
   - ❑ c. far away from Great Britain.

5. The British government chose Australia as a penal colony at the suggestion of
   - ❑ a. Captain Cook.
   - ❑ b. John Banks.
   - ❑ c. King George III.

Understanding Ideas

6. From the passage, one can infer that the aborigines did not
   - ❑ a. use tools.
   - ❑ b. eat animal meat.
   - ❑ c. have advanced industrial development.

7. One can infer from the passage that the large number of refugees to Australia during the twentieth century was probably the result of
   - ❑ a. environmental disaster.
   - ❑ b. war.
   - ❑ c. unemployment.

8. When Europeans began a colony in Australia, the aborigines
   - ❑ a. were enslaved.
   - ❑ b. were forced to leave.
   - ❑ c. caught diseases from the new arrivals.

9. Which of the following statements best expresses the main idea?
   - ❑ a. Immigrants have traveled all over the world to escape war, famine, and persecution.
   - ❑ b. After World War II, many Europeans came to Australia to rebuild their lives.
   - ❑ c. Through immigration, Australia has developed into a country with a unique and diverse culture.

10. The gold rush changed Australia's culture by
    - ❑ a. fostering the interaction of people from different backgrounds.
    - ❑ b. increasing trade.
    - ❑ c. forcing the aborigines to move.

Australia Day

Each year on January 26, Australia has its most important national holiday: Australia Day. It marks the date on which Captain Arthur Phillip and his First Fleet landed in 1788 to start the first permanent European settlement. In the past, people raised flags and took part in other events to show their patriotism. The day was also a time to recognize the accomplishments of Australia's people.

Over the years, Australia Day has gone through some modifications. Today it is a community event that celebrates the features that set the island nation apart from other countries. People show their love for their land. They honor the enduring culture of the country's aborigines. They also give thanks for the freedom they enjoy. This day also honors diversity. Australians remind the world that their home is a place where people of different races and faiths accept, and try to learn from, one another.

On Australia Day, many groups hold ceremonies. Events include parades, contests, and fireworks. People wear costumes to make themselves look like native animals or figures from the past, such as Captain James Cook. Parade marchers throw sweets to children, while music plays and people dance. In some cities, there are pie-eating contests and sports competitions. Australia Day is truly a holiday that has something for everyone.

1. **Recognizing Words in Context**

   Find the word *modifications* in the passage. One definition below is closest to the meaning of that word. One definition has the opposite or nearly the opposite meaning. The remaining definition has a completely different meaning. Label the definitions C for *closest*, O for *opposite or nearly opposite*, and D for *different*.

   _____ a. continuations

   _____ b. travels

   _____ c. changes

2. **Distinguishing Fact from Opinion**

   Two of the statements below present *facts*, which can be proved. The other statement is an *opinion*, which expresses someone's thoughts or beliefs. Label the statements F for *fact* and O for *opinion*.

   _____ a. The First Fleet carried convicts.

   _____ b. Captain Arthur Phillip landed his ships in January.

   _____ c. Australia's land is beautiful.

3. Keeping Events in Order

Number the statements below 1, 2, and 3 to show the order in which the events took place.

_____ a. The First Fleet arrives in Australia.

_____ b. People raise flags on Australia Day to remember the landing of the First Fleet.

_____ c. People celebrate the diversity of Australia's culture on Australia Day.

4. Making Correct Inferences

Two of the statements below are correct *inferences*, or reasonable guesses. They are based on information in the passage. The other statement is an incorrect, or faulty, inference. Label the statements C for *correct* inference and F for *faulty* inference.

_____ a. People of many religions live in Australia.

_____ b. Australians are proud of their history and culture.

_____ c. The aborigines are the largest ethnic group in Australia.

5. Understanding Main Ideas

One of the statements below expresses the main idea of the passage. One statement is too general, or too broad. The other explains only part of the passage; it is too narrow. Label the statements M for *main idea*, B for *too broad*, and N for *too narrow*.

_____ a. Australia Day is an important national holiday.

_____ b. Australia Day celebrates both the nation's past and its unique culture with a variety of events.

_____ c. Australia Day is the anniversary of the day the First Fleet arrived.

Correct Answers, Part A _____

Correct Answers, Part B _____

Total Correct Answers _____

Espionage in the Cold War

During World War II, the United States and the Soviet Union had already begun to spy on each other. In 1943 a U.S. program called VENONA decoded Soviet messages that had been collected since the war started. That same year, the Soviets set up the KGB and GRU—agencies devoted to espionage.

During the war, Soviet spies tried to infiltrate the Manhattan Project. This program was working to develop the first atomic bomb. Klaus Fuchs and Theodore Hall were scientists who worked at the bomb's test site at Los Alamos, New Mexico. They passed detailed information to the Soviets. With their help, the Soviet Union built a bomb much earlier than it otherwise could have. Although Fuchs, Hall, and many other "atomic spies" were arrested, the spying continued.

In 1948 a former Communist named Whittaker Chambers revealed that Alger Hiss, a top government official, had been a Communist. Congressman Richard Nixon found a set of papers, hidden in a pumpkin at Chambers's home, that connected Hiss to illegal activities. The case spread fear that the Communists might be working to destroy the United States. As a result, spying increased.

Spies used tiny cameras and other tools that sometimes made their actions seem more like the plot of a mystery novel than those of national governments. In the divided city of Berlin, Germany, spies from the United States and England dug a tunnel beneath the Soviet sector. They could then spy on the Soviets without actually entering that sector. The Soviets also had some brilliant tactics. In 1952 a Soviet listening device was found inside the Great Seal that hung in the U.S. ambassador's office in Moscow.

Historically, spying was usually viewed as immoral. As a result, it was done secretly. This changed during the Cold War. In 1960 an American pilot, Francis Gary Powers, was captured while on a U-2 spy flight over the Soviet Union. The United States admitted that its U-2 flights were spy missions. In 1962 Powers was exchanged for a Soviet prisoner and returned home. This diplomatic solution showed that both countries now saw spying as just a type of foreign policy.

After the Soviet Union collapsed in 1991, spies were still being caught. In 1994 CIA agent Aldrich Ames was arrested for selling secrets to the Soviets in 1985. The Cold War is over, but there is no end in sight for espionage.

Reading Time _____

Recalling Facts

1. The Cold War began
   - ❏ a. in the eighteenth century.
   - ❏ b. in the 1960s.
   - ❏ c. during World War II.

2. The American program that decoded Soviet communications was called the
   - ❏ a. KGB.
   - ❏ b. VENONA.
   - ❏ c. CIA.

3. Papers that proved Alger Hiss was a Communist were found
   - ❏ a. during a U-2 spy mission.
   - ❏ b. in a pumpkin.
   - ❏ c. in Los Alamos, New Mexico.

4. The research program that developed the atomic bomb was called
   - ❏ a. VENONA.
   - ❏ b. Los Alamos.
   - ❏ c. the Manhattan Project.

5. The U-2 pilot who was caught for spying was
   - ❏ a. Aldrich Ames.
   - ❏ b. Francis Gary Powers.
   - ❏ c. Klaus Fuchs.

Understanding Ideas

6. One can infer that the Soviet Union
   - ❏ a. had no interest in developing nuclear weapons.
   - ❏ b. had no nuclear weapons program of its own.
   - ❏ c. was working, at the same time as the United States was, to develop nuclear weapons.

7. One can infer from the passage that spying after the Hiss case
   - ❏ a. ended.
   - ❏ b. continues today.
   - ❏ c. is not so common today as it was during the Cold War.

8. Before the Cold War, espionage was seen as
   - ❏ a. a legitimate branch of foreign policy.
   - ❏ b. the only way to gather information about other nations.
   - ❏ c. similar to cheating.

9. From the passage, one can infer that the most dangerous spying by those in the United States was
   - ❏ a. Powers's U-2 spy missions.
   - ❏ b. the use of listening devices in the ambassador's office.
   - ❏ c. the selling of atomic secrets to the Soviets.

10. One can infer from the passage that the name Cold War conveyed that
    - ❏ a. no actual fighting took place between the United States and the Soviet Union.
    - ❏ b. the United States and Soviet Union fought actively in arctic climates.
    - ❏ c. the period involved the development of nuclear weapons.

The Rosenberg Case

The Cold War was a time of great tension. Americans feared that Soviet spies were working to destroy the United States. In this atmosphere, anyone suspected of helping the Soviets was seen as a threat to U.S. security.

In 1950 David Greenglass was accused of spying for the Soviets while working on the Manhattan Project. He claimed that Julius Rosenberg, who was married to Greenglass's sister, Ethel, had recruited him. Greenglass said that the Rosenbergs had convinced him to reveal top-secret information. The Rosenbergs were detained and charged with conspiracy to commit espionage.

Both Rosenbergs had been Communists since the 1930s, so they seemed especially dangerous to the jury when the trial began in March 1951. On the witness stand, they declined to answer certain questions. This led the jury to be even more convinced of their guilt. The two were convicted and sentenced to death.

The Rosenbergs asked for a new trial. Respected figures such as Albert Einstein and Pope Pius XII spoke out to help them. These efforts failed. On June 17, 1953, Julius and Ethel Rosenberg became the first U.S. civilians to be executed for wartime espionage.

For years people have questioned whether the Rosenbergs were really spies. Some believe that they died because of Cold War fears of Communism. Today, though, most experts believe that they were, in fact, guilty.

1. **Recognizing Words in Context**

   Find the word *declined* in the passage. One definition below is closest to the meaning of that word. One definition has the opposite or nearly the opposite meaning. The remaining definition has a completely different meaning. Label the definitions C for *closest*, O for *opposite or nearly opposite*, and D for *different*.

   _____ a. agreed

   _____ b. regretted

   _____ c. refused

2. **Distinguishing Fact from Opinion**

   Two of the statements below present *facts*, which can be proved. The other statement is an *opinion*, which expresses someone's thoughts or beliefs. Label the statements F for *fact* and O for *opinion*.

   _____ a. Greenglass worked on the Manhattan Project.

   _____ b. Julius and Ethel Rosenberg were fairly convicted.

   _____ c. The Rosenbergs were allowed to take the stand at their trial.

3. Keeping Events in Order

Number the statements below 1, 2, and 3 to show the order in which the events took place.

_____ a. David Greenglass worked on the Manhattan Project.

_____ b. Albert Einstein expressed support for the Rosenbergs.

_____ c. The Rosenbergs were put on trial for conspiracy to commit espionage.

4. Making Correct Inferences

Two of the statements below are correct *inferences,* or reasonable guesses. They are based on information in the passage. The other statement is an incorrect, or faulty, inference. Label the statements C for *correct* inference and F for *faulty* inference.

_____ a. The Rosenberg jury was aware that Julius Rosenberg was a Communist.

_____ b. Pope Pius XII supported the Rosenbergs because they were Roman Catholic.

_____ c. The execution of the Rosenbergs was highly unusual.

5. Understanding Main Ideas

One of the statements below expresses the main idea of the passage. One statement is too general, or too broad. The other explains only part of the passage; it is too narrow. Label the statements M for *main idea,* B for *too broad,* and N for *too narrow.*

_____ a. In the Rosenberg case, two alleged Soviet spies were tried and executed.

_____ b. Cold War fears of Communism resulted in trials for espionage.

_____ c. The Rosenbergs were accused of stealing nuclear secrets from the Manhattan Project.

Correct Answers, Part A _____

Correct Answers, Part B _____

Total Correct Answers _____

The era known as the Middle Ages lasted from about A.D. 500 to 1500. It was a time of great change, marking the transition from an ancient to a modern age. Of great importance in this era was the rise of commerce. Increased trade in the latter half of the Middle Ages transformed the way people lived.

Early in the Middle Ages, people had relied on farming to survive. Most farmers produced barely enough to subsist. Improved farming methods, however, soon offered higher yields. With the crop surplus, some farmers began to market their products. The surplus enabled others to become artisans. As a result, a new system of trade emerged that was much more highly ordered than the previous system of peddling.

As trade increased, bustling sites of commerce, called towns, appeared. Those who lived in towns often had multiple jobs, such as farmer, artisan, and merchant. Whatever they produced they sold at weekly markets in the town center.

To regulate trade in the towns, merchants formed unions called guilds. Guilds controlled fair-trade practices. They fixed prices, set business hours, monitored quality, and protected members from competitors. Most guilds became powerful. They were able to pass town laws and govern the courts.

Another role of the guild was to ensure the proper training of a craftsperson. The guild established a system in which a youth served as an apprentice to a master. After years of service, the youth became a day worker or a journeyman for the master. To become a master himself, the journeyman had to present the guild with a masterpiece to prove his skill. He also had to have enough money to set up his own shop.

Aside from local commerce, long-distance trade existed within Europe and between Europe and several other continents. Traveling merchants imported luxury goods such as sugar and gold from Africa, silk and spices from Asia, and rice and perfume from the Middle East. Typically, merchants sold these goods at large seasonal fairs well attended by people from all around the region.

The rise of commerce in the Middle Ages had a lasting impact on society. It weakened the feudal system that had governed the lives of the populace for centuries. With the growth of commerce and towns, people of the Middle Ages enjoyed increased prosperity and freedom. These changes foreshadowed the further transformation of the social order in the modern era.

Reading Time _____

Recalling Facts

1. The era of great change that marked the transition from an ancient to a modern age was the
   - ❑ a. Bronze Age.
   - ❑ b. Middle Ages.
   - ❑ c. Age of Exploration.

2. Bustling sites of commerce in the Middle Ages were called
   - ❑ a. towns.
   - ❑ b. farms.
   - ❑ c. castles.

3. To regulate trade, merchants formed unions called
   - ❑ a. guilds.
   - ❑ b. fairs.
   - ❑ c. markets.

4. At seasonal fairs, traveling merchants sold
   - ❑ a. produce.
   - ❑ b. crafts from their shops.
   - ❑ c. imported luxury goods.

5. The guild established a system of training for craftsmen in which youth served as
   - ❑ a. merchants.
   - ❑ b. masters.
   - ❑ c. apprentices.

Understanding Ideas

6. As trade increased, merchants formed guilds to
   - ❑ a. promote trade with distant lands.
   - ❑ b. protect their common interests in the marketplace.
   - ❑ c. fix the time and place of seasonal festivals.

7. Compared with an apprentice, a journeyman
   - ❑ a. trained fewer students.
   - ❑ b. possessed a higher level of skill.
   - ❑ c. earned less.

8. It is likely that a merchant in the Middle Ages who peddled eggs sold them
   - ❑ a. at grocery stores.
   - ❑ b. at seasonal fairs.
   - ❑ c. at weekly markets.

9. One can infer from the passage that the success of the large seasonal fairs and the sale of imported luxury goods in the Middle Ages signaled
   - ❑ a. the wealth of the general populace.
   - ❑ b. the struggle of farmers to survive.
   - ❑ c. the decline of local markets.

10. It is likely that the modern era that followed the Middle Ages was characterized by
    - ❑ a. a rise in farming.
    - ❑ b. the continued growth of commerce.
    - ❑ c. stricter government controls.

21 B   The Evolution of Numbers in the Middle Ages

In the latter part of the Middle Ages, people in Europe began to use a new number system. Before, they had relied on roman numerals, which were letters that stood for numbers. Although roman numerals were sufficient for keeping records, they were too cumbersome to use for mathematics.

With the growth of commerce in the late Middle Ages, merchants needed new ways to perform mathematical calculations. Long-distance trade offered the people of Europe some new advances to aid them. Through most of the age, merchants used counters to tally sums. This method improved when a traveling merchant brought in a calculating device, called an abacus, from the Arab world. This tool relied on the concept of place value and units of one, tens, and hundreds.

Soon afterward, an Italian merchant introduced an Arabic number system in Europe. This system relied on the same concept as the abacus. The Indian decimal system was related to place value and units. At first, the people of Europe resisted using the new system. But with time, the ease of doing arithmetic with the new system convinced them of its value. The system soon replaced roman numerals and evolved into the system in use today throughout most of the world.

1. **Recognizing Words in Context**

   Find the word *cumbersome* in the passage. One definition below is closest to the meaning of that word. One definition has the opposite or nearly the opposite meaning. The remaining definition has a completely different meaning. Label the definitions C for *closest*, O for *opposite or nearly opposite*, and D for *different*.

   _____ a. manageable

   _____ b. burdensome

   _____ c. regular

2. **Distinguishing Fact from Opinion**

   Two of the statements below present *facts*, which can be proved. The other statement is an *opinion*, which expresses someone's thoughts or beliefs. Label the statements F for *fact* and O for *opinion*.

   _____ a. Life for merchants would have been easier if they had adopted the new decimal system earlier.

   _____ b. Doing math with roman numerals was difficult.

   _____ c. Merchants used roman numerals in the Middle Ages.

3. Keeping Events in Order

Number the statements below 1, 2, and 3 to show the order in which the events took place.

_____ a. During the Middle Ages, trade increased.

_____ b. Roman numerals were no longer sufficient for merchants' calculations.

_____ c. Merchants came to rely on innovations from other regions, such as the abacus and a decimal number system.

4. Making Correct Inferences

Two of the statements below are correct *inferences,* or reasonable guesses. They are based on information in the passage. The other statement is an incorrect, or faulty, inference. Label the statements C for *correct* inference and F for *faulty* inference.

_____ a. The need for a new number system arose with the rise of commerce.

_____ b. Trade was responsible for the introduction of a new number system in Europe.

_____ c. After the Middle Ages, no one used roman numerals anymore.

5. Understanding Main Ideas

One of the statements below expresses the main idea of the passage. One statement is too general, or too broad. The other explains only part of the passage; it is too narrow. Label the statements M for *main idea,* B for *too broad,* and N for *too narrow.*

_____ a. During the Middle Ages in Europe, people changed the way they used numbers.

_____ b. Through long-distance trade, the abacus and the decimal number system were introduced to Europe during the Middle Ages.

_____ c. As societies became more complex, people needed advanced number systems.

Correct Answers, Part A _____

Correct Answers, Part B _____

Total Correct Answers _____

Free Trade in the Global Marketplace

The past 20 years have produced great advances in technology and communications. As a result, people throughout the world have become ever more connected. This growing link between the nations and people of the world is called globalization. It is a trend that has changed ways of life around the globe.

Perhaps the most controversial change in this process is the effect of globalization on commerce. In an effort to build a global economy, most nations of the world have embraced free trade. Free trade removes certain limits imposed on global commerce to make it easier for nations to exchange goods with one another. A further aim of this process is to aid poor nations and thus reduce poverty. Globalization has indeed increased trade throughout the world, but experts disagree about its impact on the poor.

The debate about recent trends in global commerce is complex. Those who support free trade in the global market point out that competition lowers prices. Its critics argue that, without controls, such a system often harms poor nations. To some extent, both are correct. For example, in Jamaica, the import of milk from the United States had both positive and negative effects. Because the imported milk was cheaper than local milk, more poor people could drink milk and improve their nutrition. At the same time, the cheaper milk put local dairy farmers out of business. Perhaps this program caused as much harm as good.

Those who support free trade in the global market do so for a number of reasons. Studies show that when a poor nation begins trading on the global level, it reaps certain benefits. Its economy grows rapidly. Multinational corporations set up factories, which provide jobs for people. Proponents claim that these factors reduce poverty and lessen the gap between the richest and poorest nations. They believe that the globalizing trend benefits the poor.

Critics of unrestricted free trade question these conclusions. Although they agree that the global market can offer growth and jobs to poor nations, they doubt that it reduces poverty. In fact, they cite studies that show that poverty has increased as a result of the global market. In addition, the gap between rich and poor nations is growing.

Regardless of which side of the debate they are on, most experts believe that globalization has great potential to aid the poor. Both sides need to find a way to make it work.

Reading Time _____

Recalling Facts

1. The growing link between the nations and people of the world is called
   - ❑ a. globalization.
   - ❑ b. commerce.
   - ❑ c. communication.

2. A process that removes certain limits imposed on global commerce, making it easier for nations to exchange goods with one another, is
   - ❑ a. communism.
   - ❑ b. free trade.
   - ❑ c. poverty.

3. Those who support free trade in the global market claim that it
   - ❑ a. increases corporate wealth.
   - ❑ b. increases poverty.
   - ❑ c. aids the poor.

4. Critics of globalization cite studies that show that the global market has
   - ❑ a. increased poverty.
   - ❑ b. narrowed the gap between the rich and poor.
   - ❑ c. aided the poor.

5. Regardless of which side they are on, most experts believe that globalization
   - ❑ a. causes economic collapse.
   - ❑ b. reduces poverty.
   - ❑ c. has great potential to aid the poor.

Understanding Ideas

6. One can conclude from the passage that both sides of the debate agree that free trade
   - ❑ a. makes it easier for nations to exchange goods with one another.
   - ❑ b. reduces poverty.
   - ❑ c. harms poor nations.

7. From the passage, one can conclude that globalization has caused
   - ❑ a. the rise of multinational corporations.
   - ❑ b. controversy about its impact.
   - ❑ c. the growing gap between the rich and the poor.

8. A person who calls for increased regulation in the globalization of commerce is most likely
   - ❑ a. a supporter of free trade in the global market.
   - ❑ b. a critic of free trade in the global market.
   - ❑ c. the head of a large multinational corporation.

9. One can conclude that globalization has the potential to aid poor nations by improving their
   - ❑ a. cultures.
   - ❑ b. welfare systems.
   - ❑ c. economies.

10. Compared with the claims of supporters of free trade in the global market, critics' conclusions are
    - ❑ a. less hopeful.
    - ❑ b. more accurate.
    - ❑ c. harder to prove.

Greenhouse Gases and Global Warming

In recent centuries, the use of fossil fuels such as coal and oil has increased the levels of carbon dioxide in the atmosphere. This gas traps heat on Earth's surface much as a greenhouse traps the Sun's heat beneath its glass panes. For this reason, scientists call carbon dioxide and other heat-trapping gases "greenhouse gases." Most scientists think that increased levels of these gases cause global warming.

At present, rich industrial nations such as the United States and Canada release the most carbon dioxide. However, poorer nations are not far behind. Globalizing trends have aided the growth of industry. This, in turn, has caused an increase in greenhouse-gas levels.

Most experts agree that increased levels of greenhouse gases will warm the planet. They predict that the rise in temperature will have a great impact on life on Earth. Global warming may cause floods, drought, storms, disease, crop failures, and the destruction of ecosystems. In the past 100 years alone, global warming has caused ice sheets to melt, sea levels to rise, and migration patterns of birds and insects to change.

Some experts, however, refute the effects of global warming. They do not think the problem is severe. There is no way to know for sure what the impact of global warming will be. However, many scientists are working to understand this complex process.

1. **Recognizing Words in Context**

   Find the word *refute* in the passage. One definition below is closest to the meaning of that word. One definition has the opposite or nearly the opposite meaning. The remaining definition has a completely different meaning. Label the definitions C for *closest*, O for *opposite or nearly opposite*, and D for *different*.

   _____ a. disprove

   _____ b. accept

   _____ c. return

2. **Distinguishing Fact from Opinion**

   Two of the statements below present *facts*, which can be proved. The other statement is an *opinion*, which expresses someone's thoughts or beliefs. Label the statements F for *fact* and O for *opinion*.

   _____ a. Greenhouse gases trap heat on Earth's surface.

   _____ b. Scientists study possible effects of global warming.

   _____ c. Global warming is the worst environmental crisis the planet faces.

3. Keeping Events in Order

Number the statements below 1, 2, and 3 to show the order in which the events take place.

_____ a. Carbon dioxide, a greenhouse gas, traps heat on Earth's surface.

_____ b. Through the burning of fossil fuels in industry and for transportation, carbon dioxide is emitted into the atmosphere.

_____ c. Increased levels of greenhouse gases produce global warming.

4. Making Correct Inferences

Two of the statements below are correct *inferences,* or reasonable guesses. They are based on information in the passage. The other statement is an incorrect, or faulty, inference. Label the statements C for *correct* inference and F for *faulty* inference.

_____ a. Global warming will continue to have a devastating effect on the planet.

_____ b. The rise of industry may have further impact on global warming trends.

_____ c. Scientists disagree about the impact that global warming will have on life.

5. Understanding Main Ideas

One of the statements below expresses the main idea of the passage. One statement is too general, or too broad. The other explains only part of the passage; it is too narrow. Label the statements M for *main idea,* B for *too broad,* and N for *too narrow.*

_____ a. Increasing burning of fossil fuels in recent centuries has created environmental problems.

_____ b. The release of greenhouse gases into the atmosphere causes global warming, which affects life on Earth.

_____ c. Scientists study global warming to determine its impact on the planet.

Correct Answers, Part A _____

Correct Answers, Part B _____

Total Correct Answers _____

A History of Pottery

Potting is the art of making clay vessels. Pottery traditions around the world have evolved through time. Technique, form, decoration, and function vary a great deal from culture to culture.

The earliest known clay objects date back tens of thousands of years. However, it appears that people did not begin to make vessels until much later. The first potters probably pinched wet clay, rolled clay coils, pounded clay slabs, or used molds to shape the body of their vessels. It is likely that they heated their pots in open fires to make them stronger. In Japan, archaeologists uncovered what are perhaps the oldest known clay vessels. These small cooking pots date back about 12,000 years. Other digs in the African Sahara have unearthed prehistoric clay vessels as well. Experts believe that these pots, which are decorated with incised and imprinted designs, served many functions.

In ancient times, cultures throughout the world had rich pottery traditions. The ancient cultures of China, Greece, Egypt, and the Americas all produced pottery. In the Americas, ancient potters made works both for cooking and ritual. Some of the first known works are from the Amazon region. The potters carved geometric designs into their pieces. Later works from the coast of Colombia featured fiber and clay mixtures. Other inventive techniques in the region include the use of wax or gum coatings to make designs on painted pots. In more recent times, the Anasazi people of North America made their first pots from woven baskets. They covered them with clay and baked them in the sun. Not until later did the Anasazi paint the black-and-white works they are best known for.

Innovations over the past 2,000 years have had an impact on the pottery of the modern age. First, the use of pottery wheels and firing kilns increased during this era. Fewer cultures crafted their works by hand or baked them in open fires. Also, with increased trade, local traditions spread to other cultures. By far the most refined and technically advanced works of this era were Chinese porcelains. These delicate white forms soon spread to other regions of the world and influenced a number of diverse traditions.

Today's pots, often works of fine art, are highly imaginative. Although some of these pieces resemble nothing that came before, other works pay homage to the rich traditions of the past.

Reading Time _____

Recalling Facts

1. Pottery is the name given
   - ❑ a. clay tile.
   - ❑ b. clay sculpture.
   - ❑ c. clay vessels.

2. The small cooking pots, unearthed in Japan, that date back 12,000 years are perhaps
   - ❑ a. the oldest known clay vessels.
   - ❑ b. the first clay objects ever found.
   - ❑ c. the most technically advanced clay works.

3. In ancient times, cultures throughout the world
   - ❑ a. all used the same potting techniques.
   - ❑ b. had rich pottery traditions.
   - ❑ c. preferred pottery to stone or metal vessels.

4. From culture to culture, technique, form, decoration, and function
   - ❑ a. are strikingly similar.
   - ❑ b. influence one another.
   - ❑ c. vary a great deal.

5. Over the past 2,000 years, the use of pottery wheels and firing kilns has
   - ❑ a. increased.
   - ❑ b. replaced more advanced techniques.
   - ❑ c. disappeared.

Understanding Ideas

6. One can conclude from the passage that pinching wet clay, rolling clay coils, and pounding clay slabs are techniques that are used to
   - ❑ a. form vessels on a pottery wheel.
   - ❑ b. craft pots by hand.
   - ❑ c. make clay.

7. From the passage, one can conclude that, after shaping and decorating a pot, one must
   - ❑ a. heat or fire it.
   - ❑ b. cover it in wax.
   - ❑ c. bless it in a special ceremony.

8. It is likely that ancient cultures of the Americas used natural materials, such as plant fibers and wax, in their clay works so as to
   - ❑ a. conserve limited clay supplies.
   - ❑ b. ensure high heat in the firing process.
   - ❑ c. improve form and design.

9. One can conclude from the passage that pottery traditions developed
   - ❑ a. from a single origin.
   - ❑ b. from the works of many cultures over time.
   - ❑ c. from advanced technology in recent times.

10. From the passage, one can conclude that modern-day pottery is characterized by
    - ❑ a. early potting techniques.
    - ❑ b. prehistoric Japanese traditions.
    - ❑ c. innovation as well as tradition.

23　B　Maria Martinez: Reviving Pueblo Tradition

The summer of 1908 was just beginning on the San Ildefonso Pueblo in New Mexico. Maria Martinez was busy making clay pots. A man came to the house to speak with her husband, Julian, about a job at an archaeological dig. Although he was there to talk to Julian, he noticed Maria's pots and complimented her work. He invited the whole family to spend the summer at the dig site.

It was during that summer that Maria first saw a shard of black pottery. This inspired the pottery for which she later became famous. Unlike other Pueblo native pots, which were red like clay, these works were black all the way through. Over the next decade, Maria worked with Julian to replicate this old form of Pueblo pottery. Their work revived a tradition that had been lost to the Pueblo people for hundreds of years.

Maria became an accomplished potter and received awards and honors worldwide. Perhaps more important, however, was the impact of her work and fame on the people of her culture. Once she mastered the forgotten technique, the black pots became a huge success. Among her people, Maria's work inspired renewed interest in Pueblo pottery traditions. More and more people in the pueblo took up the craft. The success of their work transformed the poor pueblo and revitalized Pueblo traditions.

1. Recognizing Words in Context

Find the word *revitalized* in the passage. One definition below is closest to the meaning of that word. One definition has the opposite or nearly the opposite meaning. The remaining definition has a completely different meaning. Label the definitions C for *closest*, O for *opposite or nearly opposite*, and D for *different*.

_____ a. fought

_____ b. revived

_____ c. extinguished

2. Distinguishing Fact from Opinion

Two of the statements below present *facts*, which can be proved. The other statement is an *opinion*, which expresses someone's thoughts or beliefs. Label the statements F for *fact* and O for *opinion*.

_____ a. Maria received awards and honors worldwide.

_____ b. Maria's black pots were more beautiful than those of the ancient tradition.

_____ c. It was through Julian's work at a dig that Maria was first introduced to black pottery.

3. Keeping Events in Order

Number the statements below 1, 2, and 3 to show the order in which the events took place.

_____ a. Maria's black pottery inspired renewed interest in Pueblo pottery traditions.

_____ b. Maria and her husband worked to replicate ancient Pueblo black pottery.

_____ c. At the Pueblo dig site where her husband worked, Maria saw her first piece of black pottery.

4. Making Correct Inferences

Two of the statements below are correct *inferences,* or reasonable guesses. They are based on information in the passage. The other statement is an incorrect, or faulty, inference. Label the statements C for *correct* inference and F for *faulty* inference.

_____ a. Maria's innovation served to revive tradition.

_____ b. Maria would not have achieved fame had she not made black pottery.

_____ c. Maria's work benefited Pueblo peoples.

5. Understanding Main Ideas

One of the statements below expresses the main idea of the passage. One statement is too general, or too broad. The other explains only part of the passage; it is too narrow. Label the statements M for *main idea,* B for *too broad,* and N for *too narrow.*

_____ a. Maria Martinez's beautiful pottery received awards and honors worldwide.

_____ b. Pottery is an ancient tradition in many native cultures of the Americas.

_____ c. Maria Martinez's innovation revived a lost art, transformed her community, and revitalized Pueblo traditions.

Correct Answers, Part A _____

Correct Answers, Part B _____

Total Correct Answers _____

24 A France and the Age of Reason

In the seventeenth and eighteenth centuries, a new way of thinking was unfolding throughout Europe. This intellectual movement was known as the Enlightenment. During this era, people came to understand the world and life itself on the basis of reason rather than of faith, emotion, or superstition. Because of its basis in reason, the era is sometimes called the Age of Reason.

A group of French thinkers called the *philosophes* embodied many of the ideas of the age. Aside from reason, these thinkers valued freedom, equality, knowledge, and progress. They believed that people could gain, through reason, knowledge of the physical and social world. Then the people could use what they knew to advance individually and together.

With the recent rise of science, the thinkers of the time held reason and the methods of science in high regard. Reason was the key tool in their quest for knowledge, which could be gained solely from evidence and proof. This fact called into question the authority of faith-based religion and the Church.

Throughout the age, the French thinkers launched vicious tirades against the Church. The belief system of the Church was rooted in faith and superstition. Most thinkers in the Age of Reason believed that knowledge gained through faith or superstition was false. They also believed that such thinking was an obstacle to reason. They came to see the Church as a social ill that kept people from grasping the true nature of their world. Without this knowledge, they feared that there was no hope of reform or progress.

The chief aim of the thinkers was to inspire social and political reforms that drew on values of the time. In France people sought freedom and equal rights for all. At the time, a powerful monarchy controlled France. The monarchy, nobles, and clergy had extreme power in society. The common people had none. The government restricted the basic rights of the people, such as freedom of speech and religion. Although the people pleaded for reform, the King did little to promote these rights or to curb the social inequities of the system. The desire for freedom and equal rights was one factor that incited the French Revolution. Within a few years of the first revolt, the French government accepted the Declaration of the Rights of Man. This document secured for the French the freedoms and rights that had pervaded the Age of Reason for more than a century.

Reading Time _____

Recalling Facts

1. During the Enlightenment, people came to understand the world on the basis of
   - ❑ a. reason.
   - ❑ b. superstition.
   - ❑ c. faith.

2. The Enlightenment is sometimes called
   - ❑ a. the Era of Science.
   - ❑ b. the French Revolution.
   - ❑ c. the Age of Reason.

3. The *philosophes* were a group of French thinkers whose ideas
   - ❑ a. reflected many ideas of the age.
   - ❑ b. fought bitterly against the Enlightenment.
   - ❑ c. led a revolt against the King.

4. The belief that knowledge could be gained from evidence and proof alone called into question the authority of
   - ❑ a. the methods of science.
   - ❑ b. faith-based religion and the established Church.
   - ❑ c. the French monarchy.

5. The chief aim of the thinkers in this age was to inspire
   - ❑ a. violent revolts.
   - ❑ b. social and political reform.
   - ❑ c. a return to the Church.

Understanding Ideas

6. One can conclude from the passage that the *philosophes* turned against the Church because they believed that
   - ❑ a. the Church was too powerful.
   - ❑ b. the monarchy would punish those involved in religion.
   - ❑ c. knowledge based on faith would not bring human progress.

7. It is likely that the French thinkers sought freedom and equal rights for all because they believed these rights to be
   - ❑ a. elitist.
   - ❑ b. vital to the sciences.
   - ❑ c. an aid to human progress.

8. From the passage, one can conclude that the ideas of the Enlightenment
   - ❑ a. failed to be realized.
   - ❑ b. brought about great change.
   - ❑ c. caused violence and destruction.

9. Compared with earlier times, the Enlightenment offered
   - ❑ a. a more rational way of thinking about the world.
   - ❑ b. greater faith in the established Church.
   - ❑ c. fewer freedoms and rights for humankind.

10. It is likely that the ideas of the Enlightenment
    - ❑ a. have had no impact on modern times.
    - ❑ b. live on in modern science and politics.
    - ❑ c. have been forgotten by most.

Rousseau's *Social Contract*

Jean-Jacques Rousseau was one of the foremost French thinkers of the late Enlightenment era. His writings challenged injustice and endorsed freedom and equal rights for all. One of his best-known works was *The Social Contract*.

During Rousseau's time, there was considerable corruption in the government. The regime deprived people of the natural freedoms to which Rousseau believed all were entitled. Rousseau saw how the system denied citizens basic rights, but he also believed that government was needed to preserve order. This created a conflict for Rousseau. Could he conceive of a government that preserved order without denying citizens their basic rights?

In 1762 Rousseau attempted to answer this query in *The Social Contract*. In this work, he illustrated why it was in one's best interests to consent to the rule of government. He explained that freedom and rights were social contracts. People enjoyed these rights because the rest of society agreed that they should. He saw the social contract as a compact between citizens. The role of government was to ensure that no one person deprived others of their basic rights. Moreover, wrote Rousseau, if government failed to protect the rights of all, it lost its authority. It was the consent of citizens to be ruled that gave government its power. Rousseau saw government, too, as a party in a social contract.

1. **Recognizing Words in Context**

   Find the word *endorsed* in the passage. One definition below is closest to the meaning of that word. One definition has the opposite or nearly the opposite meaning. The remaining definition has a completely different meaning. Label the definitions C for *closest*, O for *opposite or nearly opposite*, and D for *different*.

   _____ a. opposed

   _____ b. cheated

   _____ c. supported

2. **Distinguishing Fact from Opinion**

   Two of the statements below present *facts*, which can be proved. The other statement is an *opinion*, which expresses someone's thoughts or beliefs. Label the statements F for *fact* and O for *opinion*.

   _____ a. Rousseau was the greatest writer of the Enlightenment.

   _____ b. Rousseau wrote *The Social Contract* in 1762.

   _____ c. A great deal of corruption existed in the government during Rousseau's time.

3. **Keeping Events in Order**

Number the statements below 1, 2, and 3 to show the order in which the events took place.

_____ a. Corruption existed in the French government.

_____ b. Rousseau wrote *The Social Contract* while considering the role of government.

_____ c. Rousseau was troubled that some people were denied basic rights and freedoms.

4. **Making Correct Inferences**

Two of the statements below are correct *inferences,* or reasonable guesses. They are based on information in the passage. The other statement is an incorrect, or faulty, inference. Label the statements C for *correct* inference and F for *faulty* inference.

_____ a. Rousseau believed that the social contract existed between people as well as between the government and its citizens.

_____ b. Rousseau sought to resolve the conflict between imposed governmental rule and the protection of natural rights.

_____ c. Rousseau believed that enforced rule of government robbed citizens of their freedom and rights.

5. **Understanding Main Ideas**

One of the statements below expresses the main idea of the passage. One statement is too general, or too broad. The other explains only part of the passage; it is too narrow. Label the statements M for *main idea,* B for *too broad,* and N for *too narrow.*

_____ a. The writings of the Enlightenment addressed the role of government and the basic rights of humanity.

_____ b. Rousseau saw the social contract as a compact between citizens.

_____ c. With his work *The Social Contract,* Rousseau resolved the conflict he saw between the rule of government and the rights of citizens.

Correct Answers, Part A _____

Correct Answers, Part B _____

Total Correct Answers _____

When the founders of the United States wrote the Constitution, they made no mention in it of political parties. In fact, they feared that such groups would harm the nation by splitting it into factions. Political parties today, however, play a vital role in the democratic process. They bring key issues to the attention of the public and members of government. Perhaps most important, they help to select candidates for office and then campaign for the election of these candidates. A party's chief goal is to gain power in the government. This is done by winning elections and holding office.

The first function of a political party is to unite people with similar views. Because people have so many different viewpoints, this can be a complex task. When taking a stand on an issue, a party tries to devise a compromise. It attempts to speak for the views of all of its members. The party can then propose policies that serve its members' interests.

To implement policies, a party needs to win elections and hold office. The first step is to select people to run for office. In primary elections, citizens vote to select candidates for the party of their choice. To select candidates for president and vice president, party delegates attend a national convention. There they nominate the people they want to run for office, and they plan the party platform. The platform states what the party stands for and what it hopes to achieve in office.

The next step is to campaign for the candidate's election. The party sets up offices in most cities to promote its candidates. Ads, flyers, telephone calls, and door-to-door campaigners inform voters of the party's platform and candidates. Parties work hard to get voters to go to the polls.

When election day ends, the party takes on a new role. If voters elect a party's candidates, its leaders observe the winners' actions in office to see that they work toward party goals. If the party's candidates lose, its leaders work toward gaining more power in the next election. The leaders also make sure that the public and members of government are kept informed about issues of concern. If such concern is widespread, another party is likely to address the issue. In this way, a party can affect policy without holding office. Often, for lesser-known parties, this is the only opportunity to make an impact on policy.

Reading Time _____

Recalling Facts

1. The founders of the nation feared political parties would
   - ❑ a. educate the public on vital issues.
   - ❑ b. unite voters.
   - ❑ c. harm the nation.

2. A political party's chief goal is to gain power in the government by
   - ❑ a. amassing funds.
   - ❑ b. increasing membership.
   - ❑ c. winning elections and holding office.

3. A party needs to win elections and hold office to
   - ❑ a. educate the public.
   - ❑ b. implement policy.
   - ❑ c. influence officials.

4. A statement that tells what the party stands for and what it hopes to achieve in office is called
   - ❑ a. a party platform.
   - ❑ b. the Constitution.
   - ❑ c. a campaign speech.

5. If a party does not gain office, it
   - ❑ a. works to gain more power in future elections.
   - ❑ b. recesses until the next election.
   - ❑ c. dissolves permanently.

Understanding Ideas

6. One can conclude from the passage that selecting candidates to run for office is the role of
   - ❑ a. government.
   - ❑ b. political parties.
   - ❑ c. corporations.

7. From the passage, one can conclude that, in its effort to unite people with different views, a party may
   - ❑ a. campaign for members.
   - ❑ b. change the ideas of its members.
   - ❑ c. alienate members who do not agree with the compromise.

8. It is likely that all of the following are functions of political parties except to
   - ❑ a. nominate and campaign for candidates.
   - ❑ b. hear and decide court cases.
   - ❑ c. inform the public and officials of major issues.

9. It is likely that U.S. political parties first formed to
   - ❑ a. unite citizens with shared political interests.
   - ❑ b. seize government power from officials.
   - ❑ c. divide the nation into factions.

10. Compared with an independent candidate who belongs to no party, a party candidate probably has
    - ❑ a. greater access to like-minded voters.
    - ❑ b. less campaign support.
    - ❑ c. more freedom in choosing a platform.

Third Party Successes in the Twentieth Century

The structure of the U.S. political system favors two-party rule. It is true that more than two parties exist, but it is difficult for minor parties to gain federal office. In the last century, however, third parties have had an impact on the system in important ways.

In 1912 Republicans could not agree on a candidate for president. This led some party members to form the "Bull Moose" Party. The party did not win the election, but their candidate beat the Republican rival. Of greater importance, the Democrat who won office addressed most of the issues that the "Bull Moose" Party raised.

More recently a number of third parties have formed. These include the Reform Party and the Green Party. After winning almost 20 percent of the popular vote for president, Ross Perot formed the Reform Party. Perot campaigned to reduce the government deficit. Although he did not win office, those who did addressed his issue right away.

Aside from these cases, few third parties have had a major impact on the federal level. This does not mean that their role is negligible, however. Many third parties have made huge strides at the local level. One party, called the New Party, focuses solely on reform at this level. It won more than 300 of its first 400 races across the United States.

1. **Recognizing Words in Context**

   Find the word *negligible* in the passage. One definition below is closest to the meaning of that word. One definition has the opposite or nearly the opposite meaning. The remaining definition has a completely different meaning. Label the definitions C for *closest*, O for *opposite or nearly opposite*, and D for *different*.

   _____ a. significant

   _____ b. unimportant

   _____ c. changeable

2. **Distinguishing Fact from Opinion**

   Two of the statements below present *facts*, which can be proved. The other statement is an *opinion*, which expresses someone's thoughts or beliefs. Label the statements F for *fact* and O for *opinion*.

   _____ a. The "Bull Moose" party defeated its Republican rival for president in 1912.

   _____ b. Third parties will never gain office at the federal level.

   _____ c. Ross Perot formed the Reform Party.

3. Keeping Events in Order

Number the statements below 1, 2, and 3 to show the order in which the events took place.

_____ a. In 1912 Republicans could not agree on a candidate for president.

_____ b. Members of the Republican Party formed a new party, called the "Bull Moose" Party.

_____ c. The Democrat who won office took up most of the issues that the "Bull Moose" Party raised.

4. Making Correct Inferences

Two of the statements below are correct *inferences,* or reasonable guesses. They are based on information in the passage. The other statement is an incorrect, or faulty, inference. Label the statements C for *correct* inference and F for *faulty* inference.

_____ a. The structure of the U.S. political system prevents third parties from having any impact on government.

_____ b. Even when third parties do not win office, they can affect policy in important ways.

_____ c. In many ways, it is more accurate to say that the United States has a multiparty system rather than a two-party system.

5. Understanding Main Ideas

One of the statements below expresses the main idea of the passage. One statement is too general, or too broad. The other explains only part of the passage; it is too narrow. Label the statements M for *main idea,* B for *too broad,* and N for *too narrow.*

_____ a. Political parties in the United States have important functions.

_____ b. Third parties have had important successes in the last century.

_____ c. Third parties have made huge strides on the local level.

Correct Answers, Part A _____

Correct Answers, Part B _____

Total Correct Answers _____

Answer Key

Reading Rate Graph

Comprehension Score Graph

Comprehension Skills Profile Graph

ANSWER KEY

1A	1. c	2. a	3. b	4. a	5. b	6. b	7. c	8. a	9. c	10. a
1B	1. D, C, O	2. F, F, O	3. 1, 3, 2	4. F, C, C	5. N, M, B
2A	1. b	2. c	3. a	4. b	5. c	6. c	7. b	8. a	9. b	10. b
2B	1. C, D, O	2. F, O, F	3. 2, 1, 3	4. C, C, F	5. B, N, M
3A	1. a	2. b	3. b	4. c	5. a	6. c	7. b	8. c	9. a	10. a
3B	1. C, O, D	2. F, F, O	3. 3, 2, 1	4. C, F, C	5. N, M, B
4A	1. b	2. c	3. a	4. b	5. a	6. b	7. c	8. c	9. a	10. c
4B	1. O, C, D	2. F, O, F	3. 2, 3, 1	4. C, C, F	5. M, B, N
5A	1. c	2. a	3. a	4. b	5. b	6. a	7. c	8. b	9. a	10. c
5B	1. D, C, O	2. O, F, F	3. 3, 1, 2	4. F, C, C	5. B, N, M
6A	1. a	2. a	3. c	4. b	5. b	6. c	7. a	8. b	9. c	10. c
6B	1. O, D, C	2. F, F, O	3. 2, 1, 3	4. C, F, C	5. B, M, N
7A	1. b	2. c	3. a	4. c	5. a	6. b	7. c	8. b	9. a	10. b
7B	1. C, O, D	2. F, O, F	3. 1, 3, 2	4. F, C, C	5. B, N, M
8A	1. b	2. c	3. a	4. c	5. a	6. b	7. b	8. a	9. c	10. c
8B	1. C, D, O	2. O, F, F	3. 3, 2, 1	4. C, C, F	5. B, M, N
9A	1. a	2. c	3. b	4. a	5. c	6. b	7. a	8. c	9. b	10. c
9B	1. C, O, D	2. F, F, O	3. 1, 2, 3	4. C, F, C	5. B, N, M
10A	1. b	2. c	3. a	4. b	5. c	6. a	7. b	8. c	9. c	10. b
10B	1. O, D, C	2. O, F, F	3. 3, 1, 2	4. F, C, C	5. N, M, B
11A	1. c	2. a	3. c	4. b	5. b	6. b	7. a	8. c	9. a	10. c
11B	1. O, C, D	2. F, O, F	3. 3, 2, 1	4. C, F, C	5. B, N, M
12A	1. a	2. a	3. c	4. b	5. b	6. a	7. b	8. b	9. c	10. c
12B	1. D, C, O	2. F, F, O	3. 1, 3, 2	4. F, C, C	5. N, B, M
13A	1. c	2. b	3. a	4. a	5. b	6. c	7. c	8. a	9. b	10. b
13B	1. C, D, O	2. F, O, F	3. 3, 1, 2	4. C, C, F	5. M, B, N

14A	1. b	2. b	3. a	4. c	5. c	6. b	7. a	8. a	9. b	10. c
14B	1. C, O, D	2. O, F, F	3. 1, 2, 3	4. C, F, C	5. N, M, B					
15A	1. c	2. a	3. c	4. a	5. b	6. b	7. a	8. b	9. c	10. a
15B	1. D, C, O	2. F, F, O	3. 3, 2, 1	4. F, C, C	5. B, N, M					
16A	1. a	2. b	3. c	4. c	5. a	6. b	7. c	8. a	9. a	10. c
16B	1. C, D, O	2. F, O, F	3. 1, 3, 2	4. C, F, C	5. N, B, M					
17A	1. c	2. a	3. b	4. b	5. c	6. a	7. b	8. c	9. b	10. c
17B	1. O, D, C	2. O, F, F	3. 3, 1, 2	4. C, C, F	5. N, M, B					
18A	1. b	2. c	3. a	4. a	5. c	6. b	7. c	8. a	9. b	10. c
18B	1. C, O, D	2. F, O, F	3. S, S, B	4. F, C, C	5. M, N, B					
19A	1. b	2. c	3. b	4. c	5. b	6. c	7. b	8. c	9. c	10. a
19B	1. O, D, C	2. F, F, O	3. 1, 2, 3	4. C, C, F	5. B, M, N					
20A	1. c	2. b	3. b	4. c	5. b	6. c	7. b	8. c	9. c	10. a
20B	1. O, D, C	2. F, O, F	3. 1, 3, 2	4. C, F, C	5. M, B, N					
21A	1. b	2. a	3. a	4. c	5. c	6. b	7. b	8. c	9. a	10. b
21B	1. O, C, D	2. O, F, F	3. 1, 2, 3	4. C, C, F	5. M, N, B					
22A	1. a	2. b	3. c	4. a	5. c	6. a	7. b	8. b	9. c	10. a
22B	1. C, O, D	2. F, F, O	3. 2, 1, 3	4. F, C, C	5. B, M, N					
23A	1. c	2. a	3. b	4. c	5. a	6. b	7. a	8. c	9. b	10. c
23B	1. D, C, O	2. F, O, F	3. 3, 2, 1	4. C, F, C	5. N, B, M					
24A	1. a	2. c	3. a	4. b	5. b	6. c	7. c	8. b	9. a	10. b
24B	1. O, D, C	2. O, F, F	3. 1, 3, 2	4. C, C, F	5. B, N, M					
25A	1. c	2. c	3. b	4. a	5. a	6. b	7. c	8. b	9. a	10. a
25B	1. O, C, D	2. F, O, F	3. 1, 2, 3	4. F, C, C	5. B, M, N					

READING RATE

Put an X on the line above each lesson number to show your reading time and words-per-minute rate for that lesson.

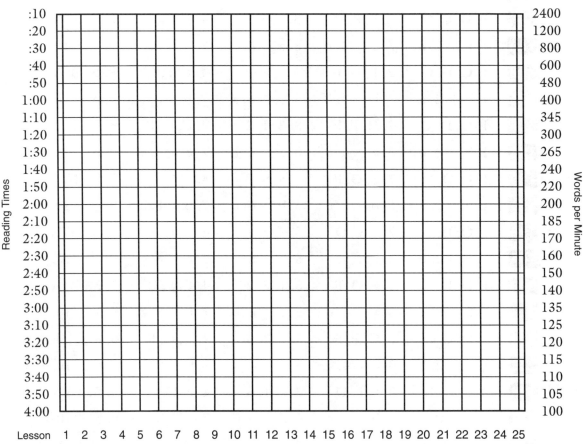

Reading Times		Words per Minute
:10		2400
:20		1200
:30		800
:40		600
:50		480
1:00		400
1:10		345
1:20		300
1:30		265
1:40		240
1:50		220
2:00		200
2:10		185
2:20		170
2:30		160
2:40		150
2:50		140
3:00		135
3:10		125
3:20		120
3:30		115
3:40		110
3:50		105
4:00		100

Lesson 1 2 3 4 5 6 7 8 9 10 11 12 13 14 15 16 17 18 19 20 21 22 23 24 25

COMPREHENSION SCORE

Put an X on the line above each lesson number to indicate your total correct answers and comprehension score for that lesson.

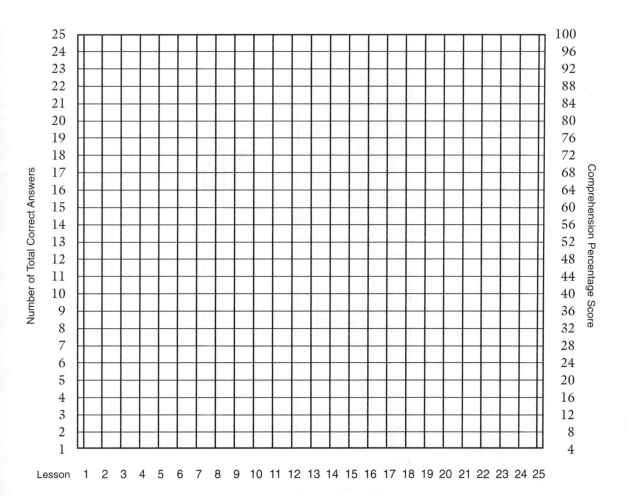

COMPREHENSION SKILLS PROFILE

Put an X in the box above each question type to indicate an incorrect reponse to any part of that question.

	Recognizing Words in Context	Distinguishing Fact from Opinion	Keeping Events in Order	Making Correct Inferences	Understanding Main Ideas
Lesson 1					
2					
3					
4					
5					
6					
7					
8					
9					
10					
11					
12					
13					
14					
15					
16					
17					
18					
19					
20					
21					
22					
23					
24					
25					